Walking with Pope Francis

The Official Documents in Everyday Language

J<small>AMES</small> H. K<small>ROEGER</small>, MM

Foreword by Cardinal Luis Antonio Tagle

ORBIS BOOKS
Maryknoll, New York 10545

Founded in 1970, Orbis Books endeavors to publish works that enlighten the mind, nourish the spirit, and challenge the conscience. The publishing arm of the Maryknoll Fathers and Brothers, Orbis seeks to explore the global dimensions of the Christian faith and mission, to invite dialogue with diverse cultures and religious traditions, and to serve the cause of reconciliation and peace. The books published reflect the views of their authors and do not represent the official position of the Maryknoll Society. To learn more about Maryknoll and Orbis Books, please visit our website at www.orbisbooks.com

Library of Congress Cataloging-in-Publication Data

Names: Kroeger, James H., author.
Title: Walking with Pope Francis : the official documents in everyday language / James H. Kroeger, MM ; with a foreword by Cardinal Luis Antonio Tagle.
Description: Maryknoll, NY : Orbis Books, [2023] | Includes bibliographical references. | Summary: "Offers overview and summary of ten of Pope Francis's principal documents"—Provided by publisher.
Identifiers: LCCN 2022038376 (print) | LCCN 2022038377 (ebook) | ISBN 9781626985131 (trade paperback) | ISBN 9781608339754 (epub)
Subjects: LCSH: Catholic Church—Doctrines. | Francis, Pope, 1936–
Classification: LCC BX1751.3 .K76 2023 (print) | LCC BX1751.3 (ebook) | DDC 230/.2—dc23/eng/20221107
LC record available at https://lccn.loc.gov/2022038376
LC ebook record available at https://lccn.loc.gov/2022038377

Contents

Foreword

A Dynamic Vision of a Renewed Church

Pope Francis, known as the "people's pope" and the "pope of mercy," begins the tenth year of his pontificate in early 2023. Born Jorge Mario Bergoglio, in Buenos Aires, Argentina in 1936, he is noted for a large number of "firsts": first Jesuit pope; first to take the name Francis; first non-European pope in more than 1,000 years; the first pope to be honored in 2013 by *Time* as "Person of the Year," the prestigious title given to the one who "has done the most to influence the events of the year."

Pope Francis, who has over forty million followers in nine languages on Twitter, is often remembered for his sense of humor and memorable quotes. When he was elected pope in 2013, he told the other cardinals: "May God forgive you for what you have done." A child once asked him if he wanted to be pope and this was his response: "You have to be totally crazy to want to be pope." Suffering from a medical condition on one of his knees, he told some visitors from Mexico that the medicine he needed for a cure was some good Mexican tequila.

His quotes contain much profound wisdom, expressed succinctly and in a memorable manner. "A little bit of mercy makes the world less cold and more just." "To be wise, use three languages: think well, feel well, and do well. And to be wise, allow yourselves to be surprised by the love of God!" We turn to exploring some of Pope Francis' pivotal insights found in his profound and pastoral writings; we draw heavily on *Evangelii Gaudium* (*The Joy of the Gospel*) [EG], Francis' first apostolic exhortation, which various writers assert is a kind of "compendium-synthesis" of his wide-ranging, visionary thought.

An Urgent Missionary Renewal. Pope Francis is constantly proposing a profound missionary transformation of the entire Church. He asserts that we need an "evangelizing Church that comes out of herself," not a Church that is "self-referential" and "lives within herself, of herself, for herself." Francis says: "I dream of a 'missionary option,' that is, a missionary impulse capable of transforming everything, so that the Church's customs, ways of doing things, times and schedules, language and structures can be suitably channeled for the evangelization of today's world rather than for her self-preservation.... All renewal in the Church must have mission as its goal if it is not to fall prey to a kind of ecclesial introversion" (EG 27).

Pope Francis continues: "Missionary outreach is *paradigmatic for all the Church's activity*.... We need to move 'from a pastoral ministry of mere conservation to a decidedly missionary pastoral ministry'" (EG 15). "I want to emphasize that what I am trying to express here has programmatic significance and important consequences.... Throughout the world, let us be 'permanently in a state of mission'" (EG 25). We seek to "put all things in a missionary key" (EG 34).

Missionary Disciples. A closely related insight of Pope Francis is that "we are all missionary disciples" (EG 119); through baptism, "all the members of the People of God have become missionary disciples" (EG 120). All Christians are "agents of evangelization." "The new evangelization calls for personal involvement on the part of each of the baptized.... Every Christian is a missionary to the extent that he or she has encountered the love of God in Christ Jesus: we no longer say that we are 'disciples' and 'missionaries,' but rather that we are always 'missionary disciples'" (EG 120).

He refers to the concept of "missionary disciples" in several other places in *Evangelii Gaudium*. "The Church which 'goes forth' is a community of missionary disciples who take the first step, who are involved and supportive, who bear fruit and rejoice. An evangelizing community knows that the Lord has taken the initiative" (EG 24). "The Church is herself a missionary disciple; she needs to grow in her interpretation of the revealed word and in her understanding of truth" (EG 40).

In discussing Church renewal, Pope Francis is following a particular approach. "What I would like to propose is something much more in line of an evangelical discernment. It is the approach of a missionary disciple, an approach 'nourished by the light and strength of the Holy Spirit'" (EG 50). "Genuine spiritual accompaniment always begins and flourishes in the context of service to the mission of evangelization.... Missionary disciples accompany missionary disciples" (EG 173).

An Encounter with Christ. Pope Francis' insights about the Church's missionary renewal come from his deep personal relationship with Christ. He writes: "I invite all Christians, everywhere, at this very moment, to a renewed personal encounter with Jesus Christ.... I ask all of you to do this unfailingly each day" (EG 3). A Christian "drinks of the wellspring of his [Jesus'] brimming heart" (EG 5). Indeed, in "this encounter—or renewed encounter—with God's love, which blossoms into an enriching friendship, we are liberated from our narrowness and self-absorption.... Here we find the source and inspiration of all our efforts at evangelization" (EG 8). "Being a Christian is not the result of an ethical choice or a lofty idea, but the encounter with an event, a person, which gives life a new horizon and a decisive direction" (EG 7); cf. Benedict XVI.

Joy: A Convincing Sign. For Pope Francis, salvation history is a "great stream of joy" (EG 5) which we must also enter. Let the joy of faith be revived, because God's mercies never end (cf. EG 6). Unfortunately, "there are Christians whose lives seem like Lent without Easter" (EG 6). "An evangelizer must never look like someone who has just come back from a funeral" (EG 10). We must *not* become "querulous and disillusioned pessimists, 'sourpusses'" (EG 85). "We feel that we must disagree with those prophets of doom" (cf. Saint John XXIII). "May the world of our time, which is searching, sometimes with anguish, sometimes with hope, be enabled to receive the good news not from evangelizers who are dejected, discouraged, impatient or anxious, but from ministers of the Gospel whose lives glow with fervor, who have first received the joy of Christ" (EG 10; cf. *Evangelii Nuntiandi* [EN] 75). We all must *not* "end up stifling the joy of mission" (EG 79).

Dedicated Service of People. Pope Francis exhorts Christ's followers to be "persons of the people" and to identify with those they serve. A true Christian is close to the people he or she serves; one does not put oneself "above" others; one remains humble. One does not seek to project a "false image," pretending to be someone other than one's true self. This humble attitude is reflected in the episcopal "motto" that Pope Francis has chosen for himself: "*miserando atque eligendo*" (lowly but chosen). He sees his own call as patterned on the call of Saint Matthew (Mt 9:9–13), who was a tax-collector and a sinner, yet called as one of Jesus' chosen twelve disciples.

Pope Francis notes that Jesus went around the towns and villages of Israel, "teaching in their synagogues, proclaiming the Good News of the Kingdom, and curing all kinds of diseases and sickness" (Mt 9:35). He paid attention to everyone, especially the "little people," like the woman who donated her two small coins to the temple (Mk 12:41–44) or the poor widow of Nain (Lk 7:11–17). Jesus truly served the "little, lost, least, lonely, and last." Service of the needy was the hallmark of Jesus' ministry—to be imitated by all of His missionary-disciples. Probably one of the most-quoted sayings of Pope Francis is: "Let us never forget that authentic power is service"; he first said this on March 19, 2013, during the inauguration of his papal ministry.

Fostering a Vatican-II Church. Pope Francis is known for many unique and symbolic actions. One such move was his decision to canonize *three* popes: John XXIII, Paul VI, and John Paul II. The action recognized the virtues and holiness of these contemporary Church leaders; it is also noteworthy that these three "pope-saints" were all active participants in the Second Vatican Council (1962–1965). It can be asserted that Pope Francis has not simply canonized three "Vatican II popes"; he has also "canonized" the legacy of the Second Vatican Council as the fundamental direction needed for the ongoing renewal of the Church.

Certainly, Pope Francis aligns himself with Vatican II which asserted that "the joys and the hopes, the griefs and the anxieties of the people of this age, especially those who are poor or in any way afflicted, these are the joys and the hopes, the griefs and the anxieties of the followers of Christ" (GS 1). He often reiterates what he told the Church in Buenos Aires, that he prefers a Church that is "bruised, hurting and dirty because it has been out on the streets, rather than a Church which is unhealthy from being confined and from clinging to its own security." He untiringly promotes a renewed Church that emerges from the Spirit-inspired vision of Vatican II.

Dynamic Evangelization. Pope Francis frequently quotes his predecessor Pope Paul VI who said that the Church must always practice a "double fidelity" both to "a message whose servants we are and to the people to whom we must transmit it" because this dual task "is the central axis of evangelization" (EN 4). Pope Francis constantly seeks to integrate fidelity with renewal and adaptability. Succinctly stated, this vision recognizes that the Church and her members need ongoing renewal; all evangelizers need to be constantly evangelized themselves. There is a traditional Latin phrase that validly describes the Church: *ecclesia semper reformanda* (Church always needing renewal and conversion). Indeed, individually and as a community we need constant renewal and updating.

For Pope Francis, this means conversion to being a poor Church that serves the poor; it means going forth "from our own comfort zone in order to reach all the 'peripheries' in need of the light of the Gospel" (EG 20). It means making mercy a central virtue in the Church's life. Quoting Saint Thomas Aquinas, Francis has said that "mercy is the greatest of all the virtues" (EG 37); this implies the qualities of tenderness, compassion, sensitivity, and caring. For Francis, Jesus is "mercy-made-flesh" (MV 24); God's mercy is incarnate in Jesus! "The Son of God, by becoming flesh, summoned us to the revolution of tenderness" (EG 88). Indeed, the name of God is mercy! This mercy is reflected in Jesus' beatitudes (Mt 5:3–12), which, according to Pope Francis, "contain the 'identity card' of a Christian because they outline the face of Jesus himself, his way of life" (January 29, 2020).

Additional Insights. Friends, these few pivotal themes introduce us to some of Pope Francis' reflections on the Church today. Yet, there are countless other topics that reflect the engaging vision of Pope *Franciscus*. He has written and spoken creatively on migrants, youth, faith, ecology, prayer, friendship, accompaniment, family, synodality, priesthood, popular piety, Mary, Saint Joseph, and the numerous challenges facing evangelization today (e.g., consumerism, complacency, throw-away culture, relativism, violence, poverty, indifference, greed, narcotics, etc.). Listing these many topics can serve as an invitation to read the well-crafted, popular summaries that form the contents of this book you hold in your hands. I assure you that your faith and life will be marvelously enriched!

These succinct popularizations introduce us to the engaging vision of Pope Francis in summary form; thus, we are truly grateful to the author for his dedicated labors. Hopefully, as you peruse these materials, you will discover that they are "appetizers" for the full writings of Pope Francis. May you also discover the vibrant "missionary spirit" of Pope Francis; he firmly believes that "Challenges exist to be overcome! Let us be realists, but without losing our joy, our boldness and our hope-filled commitment. Let us not allow ourselves to be robbed of missionary vigor" (EG 109). Again, Pope Francis personally exhorts us: "Let us not allow ourselves to be robbed of missionary enthusiasm" (EG 80).

Cardinal Luis Antonio Tagle, D.D.

Introduction

Pope Francis, chosen as the 266th pope of the Catholic Church in 2013, was the first pontiff to ever take the name of Francis, honoring the famous saint from Assisi. He is now in his tenth year of service to the Church and the wider world. During this decade, he has enriched the Church with numerous insights on a broad range of topics, including climate change, refugees and migrants, interfaith dialogue, mercy and compassion, the liturgy, and the rediscovery of the wisdom of the Second Vatican Council. His corpus of teaching, pastoral guidance, and spiritual reflection is a marvelous treasure.

The insights of Pope Francis must not remain a "hidden treasure!" Yet it may validly be asked how one can discover these multiple gems. The pathway chosen for this book is to do a popularized synthesis of ten pivotal documents, recognizing that most people will not read the original writings, due to their length and sometimes daunting language. These condensed presentations of Francis' thought seek to make his material easily accessible; they aim to faithfully capture the central insights of the papal documents and communicate them in ordinary language.

Ten items are chosen, spanning the years from 2013 to 2022. They include three encyclicals, five apostolic exhortations, and two apostolic letters. The length of the summary popularizations is only about 10 percent of the originals. Admittedly, some of the nuances of Francis' pivotal thought may get lost; readers can return to the full documents if further depth and clarity are desired. One may validly assert that Francis has served us a fine banquet or smorgasbord;

WALKING WITH POPE FRANCIS

these presentations are only the appetizers. A brief, paragraph-long overview of the ten "Francis delicacies" now follows.

• *The Light of Faith* (*Lumen Fidei*) [2013] is Francis' first encyclical, though he admits that much of the text was composed by his predecessor Pope Benedict XVI. Numerous rich insights into the dynamics of faith are found here. Readers are encouraged to make their personal journey of faith within their individual and communal state of life (single, married, poor, migrant, elderly, etc.). All can look to the great panorama of Christian examples (e.g., Saint Paul, Damien the Leper, Mother Teresa, Virgin Mary) as icons of faith, guiding us all in our ongoing faith journey.

• Francis' first apostolic exhortation is the lengthy *The Joy of the Gospel* (*Evangelii Gaudium*) [2013]; it reaches over 50,000 words. The document presents a full panorama of Francis' theology, spirituality, and vision of pastoral-missionary ministry. Many of the seminal insights found here receive further elaboration in the pope's later writings. A clear missionary tone marks the presentation; here is the origin of the widely used term that all Christians are "missionary disciples." Francis comments on the numerous contemporary challenges facing the proclamation of the Gospel today, yet he emphatically asserts, "Let us not allow ourselves to be robbed of missionary vigor" (EG 109).

• *The Face of Mercy* (*Misericordiae Vultus*) [2015] is a papal "bull," a kind of official letter or message. Here Francis is declaring an Extraordinary Jubilee Year of Mercy to commemorate the fiftieth anniversary of the closing of the Second Vatican Council (1962–1965). He believes that the Church has an urgent duty to keep the Council alive, a theme he repeatedly emphasizes on numerous occasions. With the Council the Church entered "a new phase of her history" (MV 4); it is marked by an emphasis on mercy and compassion in all of her apostolic endeavors. Personally, Francis has incorporated the theme of mercy into his papal motto, *Miserando atque eligendo* (Chosen through mercy).

• Possibly the most widely read and quoted document of Pope
Francis is his *Laudato Sí* (*On Care for Our Common Home*) [2015].
This lengthy encyclical focuses entirely on the environment. For
Francis, an ecological commitment is a moral and spiritual concern,
moving beyond ordinary matters of science, economics, and politics.
Francis wishes to engage in a "dialogue with all people about our
common home" (LS 3); he emphasizes the urgent need for an
"integral ecology." Humanity has much to learn from the vision of
Jesus and Francis of Assisi; we must consider how environmental
degradation particularly impacts the world's most vulnerable people.
Urgent action is required; the world needs a renewed relationship
with God, ourselves, one another, and all creation.

• Drawing on the 2014 and 2015 worldwide bishops' synods on
the family, *Amoris Laetitia* (*The Joy of Love*) [2016] focuses on the
concrete realities of families today, since Francis believes that "the
welfare of the family is decisive for the future of the world and that
of the Church" (AL 31). Running to over 250 pages, this apostolic
exhortation explores a vast range of topics, including the Church's
teaching on marriage and the family, people in irregular situations,
and homosexuality. One is struck by Francis' pastoral tone of love,
tenderness, and compassion for married people and their families. In
all situations and contexts, "the Church is commissioned to proclaim
the mercy of God, the beating heart of the Gospel" (AL 309).

• *Gaudete et Exsultate* (*Rejoice and Be Glad*) [2018] is the third
apostolic exhortation issued by Pope Francis. This medium-length
document is a call to holiness of life; it clearly echoes the same
summons found in *Lumen Gentium* (39–42), the document on the
Church from Vatican II. Since there are many pathways and forms
of holiness, each person is invited to discover one's unique road
of sanctity, following Jesus' life and teaching, especially the Beatitudes (Mt 5:3–12). One seeks to integrate the spiritual attitudes of
perseverance, patience, joy, boldness, passion, and a healthy sense of
humor. While we can draw inspiration from the saints and Mary,

the journey is uniquely personal. We take courage from Jesus' advice
to his disciples (Mt 5:12) to "rejoice and be glad"—in the midst of
life's trials and challenges, its joys and blessings.

• The October 2018 Synod of Bishops explored the theme
"Young People, the Faith and Vocational Discernment"; it provided
resource material for Pope Francis' apostolic exhortation *Christus
Vivit* (*Christ Lives*) [2019]. This profound document has a clear
emphasis on Christ; Francis boldly asserts, "Christ is alive and he
wants you to be alive" (CV 1). Written with Francis' characteristic
tone of frankness, simplicity, tenderness, and warmth, one senses
a distinct invitation for the Church, particularly in her youth and
pastoral ministry, to become a loving and serving community. All
are invited to personally "encounter each day your best friend, the
friend who is Jesus" (CV 151). Francis speaks from his heart to our
hearts, inviting us to become "open-hearted" missionary-disciples.

• *Querida Amazonia* (*Beloved Amazon*) [2020] emerges from
a unique bishops' synod, one that focused on a distinct ecological
territory, rather than on a particular thematic topic. Amazonia
covers nine countries, with 34 million inhabitants, including 3
million indigenous people from nearly 400 ethnic groups. Francis
structures his presentation around his "four dreams" for Amazonia;
they are social, cultural, ecological, and ecclesial. In an artistic and
literary manner, Francis often employs original indigenous poetry
to express his thoughts and dreams. One senses Francis' passion for
environmental and ecological stewardship, not only for Amazonia,
but for the entire world. All have a God-given mission: "the
protection of our common home" (QA 19).

• The third encyclical of Pope Francis, *Fratelli Tutti* (*On
Fraternity and Social Friendship*) [2020], draws its title from the
writings of Francis of Assisi, who declared that we are "brothers
and sisters all" (FT 8), *fratelli tutti*. This lengthy document (43,000
words) treats several key themes; among them are renewed human

relationships, peace and reconciliation, care for the earth as humanity's common home, and world religions at the service of human solidarity. Here one finds several common themes related to Pope Francis' second encyclical, *Laudato Sí*. As one continues absorbing the pope's engaging thought and insights, a deeper appreciation of Francis as a "pastoral theologian" grows. All can read Francis with a genuinely grateful heart.

• On the feast of Saints Peter and Paul on June 29, Pope Francis issued a medium-length apostolic letter with the title *Desiderio Desideravi* (*The Liturgical Formation of the People of God*) [2022]. The letter opens with a quote from Jesus' words at the Last Supper (Lk 22:15), expressing his desire to share the Paschal meal with his disciples. One finds three dominant themes in this pastoral instruction: the foundations of the Church's liturgy, the urgent need for deeper liturgical formation throughout the Church, and a focus on the art of celebrating the liturgy. In his conclusion, Francis strongly emphasizes a renewed understanding and acceptance of the entire corpus of teaching found in the sixteen documents of Vatican II, all as a deeper listening to the Holy Spirit serving unity and communion within the Church.

Friends, these brief glimpses into the ten popularized documents of Pope Francis chosen for this presentation seek to whet your appetite to delve into the enriching thought of our Holy Father. Be assured that your efforts to engage with Pope Francis will bring numerous rewards in your individual journey of faith. Your personal invitation has gone out to join a pilgrimage, to engage by "walking with Pope Francis." Please respond; *respondez s'il vous plait!* RSVP.

1

Lumen Fidei
The Light of Faith

(June 29, 2013)

Lumen Fidei (LF), Pope Francis' first encyclical, is a relatively brief document. Francis admits that Pope Benedict XVI "had almost completed a first draft of an encyclical on faith," and for this initial work "I am deeply grateful to him." Francis says that "as his brother in Christ, I have taken up his fine work and added a few contributions of my own" (LF 7). As one reads the encyclical, it becomes clear through the style and content of the document that Pope Benedict had the major input into this document. It harmonizes well with the vision Pope Benedict outlined in his proclamation of 2012 as a "year of faith." In addition, this document is meant to supplement what Benedict had previously written in his encyclicals on the virtues of charity and hope.

The structure of *Lumen Fidei* is simple and direct, containing an introduction and four chapters; it concludes with Marian reflections and a final prayer to Mary. The introduction shows how the ancients viewed faith; it narrates how the Second Vatican Council, a "Council on faith," sought to bring faith into the contemporary world. Chapter 1 shows that we believe in a God of mercy and how Christians can "see with the eyes of Jesus and share in his mind" (21).

In Chapter 2 Francis portrays the close link between faith and truth; he laments the "massive amnesia in our contemporary world" (25). The importance of evangelization and the transmission of faith are central themes of Chapter 3. Finally, in Chapter 4, Francis explains the link between faith and the common good; there are inspiring reflections on Mary's pilgrimage of faith.

Readers will be enriched by the insights into the dynamics of faith found in this document—even as they struggle to understand its dense language. They will be encouraged to continue their own personal faith journey in the family, in marriage, as youth, with the poor and marginalized, in the Church. Faith needs to be appreciated for the significant contribution that it can make to a contemporary society tempted to fall into new forms of idolatry. The encyclical strikes a positive note as it unfolds how people through the centuries have lived their faith (e.g., Abraham, Moses, Saint Paul, Francis of Assisi, Mother Teresa of Calcutta, and the Virgin Mary). Faith, indeed, is a special gift that we pray may be granted to us, making us icons of faith to others.

Lumen Fidei
Synthesis Text

INTRODUCTION

The Light of Faith (1). Jesus brought us the great gift of faith, a great light. The pagan world had the cult of the sun god, *Sol Invictus*; however, the risen Christ is the true light of the world (Jn 8:12), the morning star that never sets. **An Illusory Light? (2–3). (2).** Some contemporaries object to speaking of the light of faith; they protest (e.g., Nietzsche), asserting that Christianity diminishes the full meaning of human existence. **(3).** In this view, faith is associated with darkness; faith becomes a leap in the dark. However, when there is absence of light, everything becomes confused; life moves in endless circles, going nowhere.

A Light to Be Recovered (4–7). **(4).** Today it is urgent to appreciate that faith is a light; when faith is gone, all other lights begin to dim. Dante in the *Divine Comedy* affirms that faith is a burning flame and a heavenly star. **(5).** Pope Benedict proclaimed a year of faith (2012) to renew our appreciation of the wonders faith brings. The deep faith of the early Christians prepared them to bear public witness—even to giving their life. **(6).** The Year of Faith celebrated the fiftieth anniversary of the opening of Vatican II (1962–1965), which was "a Council on faith," showing how faith enriches life in all its dimensions. **(7).** Benedict had already begun this document on faith; it was meant to complement his earlier encyclicals on charity (*Caritas in Veritate*) and hope (*Spe Salvi*), a trilogy on the three theological virtues (cf. 1 Cor 13:13).

CHAPTER ONE: WE HAVE BELIEVED IN LOVE (cf. 1 Jn 4:16)

Abraham, Our Father in Faith (8–11). **(8).** Faith opens the pathway before us; we see Abraham as our "Father in Faith." He personally responded to God's Word. **(9).** The word spoken to Abraham is both a call and a promise; it is closely bound up with hope in the future. **(10).** As a man of faith, Abraham gains strength by putting his life in the hands of the God who is faithful. **(11).** Abraham recognizes a profound call; God asks him for complete trust, to believe he is the source of life. Undoubtedly, the great test of Abraham's faith is the challenge to sacrifice his own son, Isaac.

The Faith of Israel (12–14). **(12).** Israel's faith, following that of Abraham, is narrated in the Book of Exodus; concrete stories of life manifest this journey of faith. **(13).** Israel is tempted to unbelief, and the people yield more than once. They reverence idols, the work of their own hands; they refuse to be constantly transformed and renewed by God's call. **(14).** Moses intercedes for the people; they come to realize that "faith is God's free gift, which calls for humility and the courage to trust and to entrust." It is an invitation to an encounter with God.

The Fullness of Christian Faith (15–18). (15). Faith is centered on the risen Christ and the love he personally has for each of us (1 Jn 4:16); succinctly stated, "Christian faith is thus faith in a perfect love, in its decisive power, in its ability to transform the world and to unfold its history." **(16).** The clearest proof of Christ's love is his voluntary death for all humanity (Jn 15:13); it is precisely in contemplating Jesus' death that faith grows stronger. **(17).** We can appreciate the utter reliability of God's love through faith in the resurrection. We agree with Saint Paul: "If Christ has not been raised, your faith is futile" (1 Cor 15:17); we personally possess "faith in the Son of God, who loved me and gave himself for me" (Gal 2:20). **(18).** Our faith in Christ also intimately unites us to Christ, thus strengthening our faith; we personally welcome him into our lives, cling to his love, and follow in his footsteps.

Salvation by Faith (19–21). (19). In accepting the gift of faith, believers become a new creation; they become God's children and personally, in imitation of Jesus, say, "Abba, Father" (Rom 8:15). Our salvation by faith is not our own doing; it is "the gift of God" (Eph 2:8). **(20).** Faith is centered on Christ, for by his incarnation and resurrection, he has embraced all human life and history; faith gives us the light to illumine both the origin and the end of life. **(21).** We appreciate the difference that faith makes for us; our lives are enlarged and expanded. We begin to see things with the love and vision of Jesus. **The Ecclesial Form of Faith (22).** Believers live their lives in the Church; they see themselves in the light of the faith they profess. Faith is not only a private matter; necessarily it is ecclesial, professed from within the Body of Christ as a concrete communion of believers.

CHAPTER TWO: UNLESS YOU BELIEVE, YOU WILL NOT UNDERSTAND
(cf. Is 7:9)

Faith and Truth (23–25). (23). The Bible narrates that the prophet Isaiah tells King Ahaz, "Unless you believe, you will not understand" (Is 7:9). Truly, because God is trustworthy, it is reasonable to have faith in him and to accept his word. **(24).** We conclude that we need knowledge and truth to stand firm and move forward. "Faith without truth does not save." **(25).** This faith-truth bond is pivotal in today's age that places its trust in technology and scientific know-how. We need to counteract the "massive amnesia in our contemporary world," which forgets the ill effects of the totalitarian movements of the last century.

Knowledge of the Truth and Love (26–28). (26). We believe that Christian faith can provide an important service to promote the common good for everyone's benefit; faith enables us to see people and all reality with new eyes. **(27).** Authentic love is more than an ephemeral emotion; love requires truth so as to establish lasting bonds. Faith-filled reason and enlightened love are needed like two eyes so that we can see properly. **(28).** Thus, "faith-knowledge," born of God's love, lights up a path in history for all peoples and even the created world.

Faith as Hearing and Sight (29–31). (29). Because "faith-knowledge" is linked to the covenant, the Bible presents it as a form of hearing. Saint Paul asserts that "faith comes from hearing" (Rom 10:17); he also speaks of the "obedience of faith" (Rom 1:5; 16:26). **(30).** This bond between seeing and hearing in faith-knowledge is clearly evident in John's Gospel; the evangelist asserts that to hear is to believe. Joined to hearing, seeing becomes a form of following Christ (cf. Jn 20:8, 14, 18). Thomas Aquinas speaks of "a faith which sees." **(31).** Saint John also speaks of faith as touch:

"What we have heard, what we have seen with our eyes and touched with our hands, concerning the word of life" (1 Jn 1:1). When we touch Jesus with our heart, we come to believe; we "are configured to Jesus and receive the eyes needed to see him."

The Dialogue between Faith and Reason (32–34). (32). Christian faith opens us to the power of God's total love and penetrates the core of our human experience. Pope John Paul II showed how faith and reason strengthen each other (*Fides et Ratio* 61–62); the light of faith illumines all our human relationships. **(33).** Saint Augustine integrated hearing and seeing; he says that in the end we will see and we will love. **(34).** Love penetrates our heart. The believer knows that we do not possess the truth; rather, it is God's truth that embraces and possesses us.

Faith and the Search for God (35). The light of faith assists us in our dialogue with the followers of other religions. The religious person sees God in daily life experiences, the cycle of the seasons, the earth's fruitfulness, and the movement of the cosmos. The deeper a Christian is immersed in Christ's light, the better he can accompany others on the path toward God. **Faith and Theology (36).** Theology is impossible without faith; theology demands the faith and humility to be "touched" by God, while admitting one's limitations before the mystery. Theology also has an ecclesial form; it integrates with the Church's magisterium.

CHAPTER THREE: I DELIVERED TO YOU WHAT I ALSO RECEIVED (cf. 1 Cor 15:3)

The Church, Mother of Our Faith (37–39). (37). Those who have received the gift of faith cannot keep this treasure to themselves. They reflect God's light to others, just as the light from the Paschal candle lights countless other candles. **(38).** The transmission of the faith to men and women everywhere comes through an unbroken chain of witnesses; it is received through the memory and witness of others. The Church, as a mother, guides us along our pilgrimage of faith. **(39).** We cannot believe simply on our own; faith is not an individual decision. We need the communion of the Church; we discover that we are not alone. We always pray, saying, "Our Father."

The Sacraments and the Transmission of Faith (40–45). (40). The Church, similar to a family, passes on her entire store of memories to her children, assisted by the Holy Spirit; this reality was confirmed by the Second Vatican Council (cf. *Dei Verbum* 8). The special means to hand on her living Tradition are the sacraments; they communicate "an incarnate memory." **(41).** Faith transmission occurs first and foremost in Baptism, whereby we become a new creation and God's adopted children. This is not the act of an isolated individual; no one baptizes himself. **(42).** Various aspects of Baptism introduce us to the Church's teaching: for example, Trinitarian formula, immersion in life-giving water, and so on. The recipient is filled with the power of Christ's love and prepared for the journey of life. **(43).** Receiving a new name and a new life, the recipient begins life within the community of the Church; this will be further strengthened in the sacrament of Confirmation. **(44).** The sacramental character of faith finds its highest expression in the Eucharist. **(45).** The Church hands down her memory, particularly through the profession of faith; it has a Trinitarian structure and a confession of all the mysteries of Christ's life up to his death, resurrection, and ascension. Truly, faith is a journey of communion with the living God.

Faith, Prayer, and the Decalogue (46). The storehouse or treasury of the Church's memory is composed of four pivotal elements: the profession of faith expressed in the Creed, the celebration of the sacraments, the Ten Commandments or

Decalogue, and prayer, particularly the Our Father. Further elaboration is found in the *Catechism of the Catholic Church*.

The Unity and Integrity of Faith (47–49). (47). The Church's unity is linked to unity in faith: "there is one body and one Spirit… one faith" (Eph 4:4–5). Saint Leo the Great says, "If faith is not one, then it is not faith." Faith is also one, as it is grounded in the concrete event of the incarnation; in addition, faith is one because it is shared by the whole Church. **(48).** Since faith is one, it needs to be professed in its purity and integrity; thus, the Church is vigilant, assuring that the deposit of faith is transmitted in its entirety. Truly, the faith is universal and catholic. **(49).** As a service to the unity of the faith and its integral transmission, the Lord has endowed the Church with the gift of apostolic succession.

CHAPTER FOUR: GOD PREPARES A CITY FOR THEM
(cf. Heb 11:16)

Faith and the Common Good (50–51). (50). Scripture highlights the faith of the patriarchs and righteous men and women of the Old Testament, for example, Noah and Abraham. Their faith rests in God's fidelity; they possess interior firmness and steadfast conviction; faith enlightens their human relationships. **(51).** Linked to God's love, the light of faith serves justice, law, and peace; it enhances human relationships. In a word, "Faith is truly a good for everyone; it is a common good."

Faith and the Family (52–53). (52). The first area that faith enlightens in our human journey is the family; it begins with the stable union of man and woman in marriage. We appreciate the goodness of sexual differentiation, whereby spouses can become one flesh (cf. Gen 2:24) and are enabled to give birth to new human life. **(53).** Family and faith facilitate growth at every stage of life: childhood, youth, adulthood, retirement. Faith enhances all stages of our life, yet we recall that "faith is no refuge for the fainthearted."

A Light for Life in Society (54–55). (54). The family deepens one's faith, making it a light that illumines all our relationships in society. Faith teaches us to see every human person as a blessing; it enables us to find our place in the universe. **(55).** In addition, faith reveals the love of God the Creator, enabling us to respect nature all the more. If faith is weakened, the foundations of life also risk being weakened. In a word, faith illumines all life and society.

Consolation and Strength amid Suffering (56–57). (56). The Psalmist says, "I kept my faith, even when I said, 'I am greatly afflicted'" (Ps 116:10). Faith often involves speaking of painful testing, yet we know that it is in weakness and suffering that we discover God's power and love. **(57).** Faith does *not* make us forget the world's suffering; this is seen in the life of Saint Francis of Assisi and the leper and in Blessed Mother Teresa of Calcutta and her poor. Faith engenders hope, and "hope does not disappoint" (Heb 11:10). In union with faith and charity, hope propels us toward a sure future.

Blessed Is She Who Believed (Lk 1:45). (58–60). (58). Mary is the perfect icon of faith; as Saint Elizabeth says, "Blessed is she who believed" (Lk 1:45). Mary typifies the many faithful women of the Old Testament, completing her own pilgrimage of faith, following in the footsteps of her own son. **(59).** Because of her intimate bond with Jesus, Mary is connected to our faith. She accompanies Jesus to the cross (Jn 19:25); her motherhood is extended to each of Jesus' disciples (Jn 19:26–27). She accompanies the disciples, imploring the gift of the Spirit (Acts 1:14). **(60).** We turn in prayer to Mary, Mother of the Church and Mother of our faith: Mother, help our faith. Help us to believe when we stand beneath the shadow of the cross. Sow in our faith the joy of the risen One. Remind us that those who believe are truly never alone. May this light of faith always increase in us.

2

Evangelii Gaudium
The Joy of the Gospel

(November 24, 2013)

Evangelii Gaudium (EG), Pope Francis' first apostolic exhortation, is lengthy—over 50,000 words. Here Francis is proposing a profound missionary renewal of the entire Church, desiring a truly evangelizing Church. Francis says, "I dream of a 'missionary option,' that is, a missionary impulse capable of transforming everything" (27). He asserts, "All renewal in the Church must have mission as its goal if it is not to fall prey to a kind of ecclesial introversion" (27). He believes, "Missionary outreach is *paradigmatic for all the Church's activity*" (15). It is noteworthy that Francis completed EG within eight months of his election as pope. It is dated November 24, 2013, feast of Christ the King; it commemorates the conclusion of the Year of Faith.

One may validly assert that this document summarizes the pope's theology, spirituality, and vision of pastoral-missionary ministry. His desire that the Church be "permanently in a state of mission" (25) comes from his deep personal relationship with Christ, and he invites "all Christians, everywhere, at this very moment, to a renewed personal encounter with Jesus Christ" (3). A pivotal insight of Francis is that "we are all missionary disciples"

(119); "we no longer say that we are 'disciples' and 'missionaries,' but rather that we are always 'missionary disciples.'" (120) "Missionary disciples accompany missionary disciples" (173). Evangelizers' lives must "glow with fervor" since they have received "the joy of Christ" (10).

Pope Francis reveals his sense of humor at several points. He notes that, unfortunately, "there are Christians whose lives seem like Lent without Easter" (6). "An evangelizer must never look like someone who has just come back from a funeral" (10). We must *not* become "querulous and disillusioned pessimists, 'sourpusses'" (85). Quoting Saint John XXIII, Francis asserts, "We feel that we must disagree with those prophets of doom" (84).

In EG Pope Francis makes following Jesus as his disciple an attractive and welcomed invitation; this holds true because "being a Christian is not the result of an ethical choice or a lofty idea, but the encounter with an event, a person, which gives life a new horizon and a decisive direction" (8); see Benedict XVI. Francis provides copious insights into various challenges facing the proclamation of the Gospel today, mentioning consumerism, complacency, blunted consciences, relativism, secularist rationalism, violence, poverty, indifference, greed, and narcotics. Yet he remains realistically optimistic, asserting, "Challenges exist to be overcome! Let us be realists, but without losing our joy, our boldness, and our hope-filled commitment. Let us not allow ourselves to be robbed of missionary vigor" (109)!

Evangelii Gaudium
Synthesis Text

INTRODUCTION

The Joy of the Gospel (1). Gospel joy fills the hearts and lives of those who encounter Jesus; the Church is invited to embark on renewed evangelization marked by this joy.

A Joy Ever New, A Joy That Is Shared (2–8). (2). A great danger in today's world, which is pervaded by consumerism, is that it produces a covetous heart and a blunted conscience, no longer sensitive to God's voice. **(3).** All Christians are invited to a renewed, personal encounter with Jesus; his tenderness never disappoints and is always capable of restoring our joy. **(4).** Old Testament writers, particularly the prophets, abound in announcing the coming joy of salvation in messianic times. **(5).** The Gospels constantly invite us to rejoice; Mary exemplifies this joy: "My spirit rejoices in God my Savior" (Lk 1:28). **(6).** Unfortunately, "There are Christians whose lives seem like Lent without Easter." **(7).** Authentic joy is often manifest in the life of poor people. Being a Christian is the result of an encounter with the person of Christ. **(8).** This encounter with God's love liberates us from narrowness and self-absorption.

The Delightful and Comforting Joy of Evangelizing (9–13). (9). Goodness is diffusive; it makes us more sensitive to the needs of others. **(10).** The joy of Christ overflows into mission and into the life of the evangelizer; "an evangelizer must never look like someone who has just come back from a funeral." **(11).** All evangelizers need to rediscover the freshness of the Gospel; thus, "every form of authentic evangelization is always 'new.'" **(12).** We follow Jesus, "the first and greatest evangelizer"; we accept that "God asks everything of us, yet at the same time he offers everything to us." **(13).** Joy in evangelization arises from grateful remembrance, reinforced by the Church's daily celebration of the Eucharist.

The New Evangelization for the Transmission of the Faith (14–15). (14). The 2012 Synod of Bishops focused on the theme of new evangelization, including emphases on pastoral ministry, lukewarm Christians, and those who do not know Christ. How can the Church attract them? **(15).** Missionary engagement is a challenge to the Church; it must become paradigmatic for all the Church's activity.

The Scope and Limits of This Exhortation (16–18). (16). Pope Francis willingly writes this document after the 2012 synod, yet he does not wish to usurp the role of local bishops; he also wishes to promote a sound decentralization. **(17).** Francis chooses to focus on seven areas that will guide the Church in this new phase of evangelization. **(18).** The pope proposes a definite style of evangelization that should transform all Church activities; in everything the Church seeks to reflect Gospel joy.

CHAPTER ONE: THE CHURCH'S MISSIONARY TRANSFORMATION

(19). All evangelization takes place in obedience to the missionary mandate of Jesus. **A Church That Goes Forth (20–23). (20).** All Christians and every community are called to participate in mission, going forth from their comfort zone and reaching the peripheries. **(21).** The Church as the community of Jesus' disciples always goes forth with missionary joy. **(22).** God's word will be manifested in unpredictable ways that surpass our calculations and ways of thinking. **(23).** Communion and mission are profoundly interconnected; the joy of the Gospel excludes no one.

Taking the First Step, Being Involved and Supportive, Bearing Fruit and Rejoicing (24). The Church, a community of missionary disciples and an evangelizing community, seeks to take on "the smell of the sheep," attracting sheep to hear its voice. **Pastoral Activity and Conversion (25–26). (25).** Francis asserts that mere administration is not sufficient; throughout the world the Church must be "permanently in a state of mission." **(26).** Pope Paul VI affirmed that authentic renewal involves the entire Church; such renewal, as Vatican II affirmed, consists in a radical fidelity to her own calling.

An Ecclesial Renewal That Cannot Be Deferred (27–33). (27). Boldly, Francis asserts, "I dream of a 'missionary option,' that is, a missionary impulse capable of transforming everything." "All renewal in the Church must have mission as its goal if it is not to fall prey to a kind of ecclesial introversion." **(28)**. The parish serves as a fine venue for hearing God's Word, growth in Christian life, dialogue, proclamation, charitable outreach, worship, and celebration. **(29)**. The Church is enriched by basic communities, various movements, and forms of association; they should not lose contact with the local parish. **(30)**. Each particular/local church, as a portion of the Catholic Church, is the primary subject of evangelization; they should undertake a resolute process of discernment, purification, and reform. **(31)**. Every bishop is to always foster true missionary communion in his own diocese. **(32)**. The papacy and episcopal conferences necessarily are to be mission-focused, avoiding excessive centralization. **(33)**. All missionary renewal needs boldness and creativity, avoiding an attitude of "We have always done it this way."

From the Heart of the Gospel (34–39). **(34)**. Putting everything in a missionary key will affect the Church's way of communicating the message. **(35)**. Pastoral ministry in a missionary style concentrates on the essential and beautiful elements of the faith. **(36)**. The basic core of Christianity focuses on the saving love of God made manifest in Jesus Christ. Vatican II spoke of a "hierarchy of truths" affecting Church dogma and her moral teaching. **(37)**. Saint Thomas Aquinas noted that mercy is the greatest of all the virtues; it is proper to God to have mercy. **(38)**. In a balanced way, the Church must draw out the pastoral consequences of the Council's teaching. **(39)**. Above all else, Christians are asked to focus on God's love, so all will appreciate "the fragrance of the Gospel."

A Mission Embodied within Human Limits (40–45). **(40)**. The Church herself is a missionary disciple; she must constantly bring out the inexhaustible riches of the Gospel. **(41)**. The Church always seeks to express its unchanging truths in ways that express their abiding newness; Saint John XXIII observed, "The deposit of faith is one thing.... The way it is expressed is another." **(42).** Faith often seems paradoxical; it retains a certain obscurity that does not detract from the firmness of assent. **(43).** There are many beautiful customs in the Church, but they must be reexamined to ascertain if they still remain effective tools today. **(44).** All Church ministries should be accompanied with mercy and patience; "the confessional must not be a torture chamber, but rather an encounter with the Lord's mercy." **(45).** The task of evangelization has many variables; a missionary heart is aware of these diverse factors as it engages people, always ready to let "its shoes get soiled by the mud of the streets."

A Mother with an Open Heart (46–49). (46). A missionary Church has open doors and goes out to reach those on the fringes of humanity. **(47).** The Church should not close the doors of the sacraments (e.g., Baptism) for simply any reason; the Eucharist "is not a prize for the perfect but a powerful medicine and nourishment for the weak." **(48).** The whole Church takes up the missionary impulse, going forth to everyone without exception. **(49).** Francis forcefully asserts, "I prefer a Church which is bruised, hurting, and dirty because it has been out on the streets, rather than a Church which is unhealthy from being confined and from clinging to its own security."

Chapter Two: Amid the Crisis of Communal Commitment

(50). The Church as a "missionary disciple" always proceeds with "evangelical discernment" under the light of the Holy Spirit. **(51).** It is not the task of the pope to offer a complete analysis of all of contemporary reality; each community and bishops' conference has the grave responsibility to scrutinize the "signs of the times."

Some Challenges of Today's World (52). Today humanity is experiencing a turning point in its history; numerous challenges exist. **No to an Economy of Exclusion (53–54). (53).** The Church opposes an economy of exclusion and inequality as well as contemporary "throwaway culture." **(54).** Truly, trickle-down economic theories do not work, and the "globalization of indifference" has grown.

No to the New Idolatry of Money (55–56). (55). The world faces a denial of the primacy of the human person; there is the idolatry of money and the dictatorship of an impersonal economy. **(56).** Countless challenges exist, for example, widespread corruption, self-serving tax evasion; indeed, the thirst for power and possessions knows no limits. **No to a Financial System That Rules Rather Than Serves (57–58). (57).** Behind these current attitudes lurks a rejection of ethics and a rejection of God. **(58).** Stated succinctly, "Money must serve, not rule!"

No to the Inequality That Spawns Violence (59–60). (59). Violence cannot be eliminated until exclusion and inequality in society and between peoples are reversed; the world's socioeconomic system is unjust at its roots. **(60).** Inequality eventually results in violence; there is inordinate consumption and widespread corruption in numerous countries today.

Some Cultural Challenges (61–67). (61). Some Christians face persecutions and attacks on religious freedom; there is widespread indifferentism and relativism as well as the crisis of ideologies. **(62).** Important cultural roots and values are being lost today; the media often undervalue the sacredness of marriage and the stability of the family. **(63).** Christian faith faces several challenges: new religious movements, fundamentalism, and a spirituality without God. Sacraments are often administered apart from other forms of evangelization. **(64).** Moral relativism is widespread today; the Church seeks to promote both critical thinking and the development of mature moral values. **(65).** The Church is engaged in finding solutions to problems affecting peace, social harmony, the land, the defense of life, and human and civil rights. **(66).** Undoubtedly, numerous problems show that today the family is experiencing profound cultural crises. **(67).** Individualism militates against the Christian commitment to "bear one another's burdens" (Gal 6:2).

Challenges to Inculturating the Faith (68–70). (68). Christians, employing the eyes of faith, acknowledge the action of the Holy Spirit, seeing the "seeds of the word" being sown in evangelized popular cultures. **(69).** It is imperative to evangelize cultures in order to inculturate the Gospel. **(70).** Popular piety can be a fruitful starting point for handing on the faith.

Challenges from Urban Cultures (71–75). (71). The Church affirms the need to "look at our cities with a contemplative gaze," searching for God's presence in individuals and groups. **(72).** Many unique factors of cities, different from those in the countryside, require the Church's attention. **(73).** New emerging cultures can serve as "a privileged locus of the new evangelization." **(74).** Newer approaches to evangelization need to shed light on new ways of relating to God, to others, and to the world around us. **(75).** The urban reality is very complex and challenging; thus, a uniform and rigid program of evangelization must give way to creative and diverse approaches to Gospel witnessing.

Temptations Faced by Pastoral Workers (76–77). (76). Admittedly, all feel pain and shame at the sins of some members of the Church, yet this reality must never make us forget how many Christians are giving their lives in love. **(77).** Today's globalized culture presents both limits and new possibilities; deep discernment is needed.

Yes to the Challenge of a Missionary Spirituality (78–80).
(78). Some religious have an inordinate concern for their personal freedom and relaxation; this discourages the encounter with others. **(79).** Some pastoral workers even relativize or conceal their Christian identity and convictions; this stifles the joy of mission. **(80).** Such pastoral and practical relativism must be overcome; Francis asserts, "Let us not allow ourselves to be robbed of missionary enthusiasm!"

No to Selfishness and Spiritual Sloth (81–83). (81). The Church needs to recover missionary dynamism; otherwise, she falls into a state of paralysis and apathy. **(82).** Diverse factors can cause problems: unrealistic expectations, lack of patience, vain dreams of success, obsession with immediate results, nonacceptance of the cross. **(83).** "A tomb psychology thus develops and slowly transforms Christians into mummies in a museum." Francis proclaims, "Let us not allow ourselves to be robbed of the joy of evangelization."

No to a Sterile Pessimism (84–86). (84). We should view the problems of the world as challenges that can help us grow. Following Pope John XXIII's opening speech at Vatican II, we disagree with the "prophets of doom" who only see problems in today's world. **(85).** We avoid becoming "disillusioned pessimists, sourpusses"; our Christian faith accepts the cross and rejects the temptation to defeatism. **(86).** If a "spiritual desertification" results, we point the way to the Promised Land and keep hope alive. Francis offers a challenge: "Let us not allow ourselves to be robbed of hope!"

Yes to the New Relationship Brought by Christ (87–92).
(87). Christians are to take advantage of all means of human communication; this means avoiding self-enclosed and selfish choices. **(88).** Some may desire a purely spiritual Christ, without flesh and without the cross; we always remember that the Son of God, by becoming flesh, summoned us to the revolution of tenderness. **(89).** Our

challenge today is to adequately respond to many people's thirst for God; this cannot be achieved with a "disembodied Jesus who demands nothing of us with regard to others." **(90)**. Genuine forms of popular religiosity are authentic and praiseworthy; they are born of the incarnation of Christian faith in popular culture. **(91)**. In addition, they help us find Jesus in the faces of others, in their voices, in their pleas; we seek to live in deeper fraternity. **(92)**. We aspire to a mystical and contemplative fraternity, constantly seeking new ways of living together in fidelity to the Gospel. Francis asserts, "Let us not allow ourselves to be robbed of community!"

No to Spiritual Worldliness (93–97). **(93)**. Spiritual worldliness hides behind the appearance of piety and even love for the Church; however, it seeks human glory and personal well-being, not the Lord's glory. **(94)**. This worldliness is fueled in two interrelated ways: the attraction of Gnosticism (a purely subjective faith) and neo-Pelagianism (trusting one's own powers). [Note that Pope Francis extensively treats these two serious errors in Chapter 2 of *Gaudete et Exsultate*: "Two Subtle Enemies of Holiness" (sections 35–62).] **(95)**. Harmful worldliness may be manifested in various attitudes: "an ostentatious preoccupation for the liturgy, for doctrine and the Church's prestige"; this turns the life of the Church "into a museum piece or something which is the property of a select few." **(96)**. Our Church is glorious, not because of huge apostolic projects, but because of its history of sacrifice, hopes, daily struggles, and lives spent in service. **(97)**. To avoid errors the Church must constantly go out from herself, keeping focused on Jesus Christ and the poor. Francis pleads, "Let us not let ourselves to be robbed of the Gospel!"

No to Warring among Ourselves (98–101). **(98)**. There are "wars" that take place within the people of God and in various communities; these may arise from spiritual worldliness. **(99)**. Christians everywhere need to offer to the world a radiant and attractive witness of fraternal communion; we guard against the temptation of jealousy. **(100).** Francis is pained when he sees various forms of enmity, division, calumny, defamation, vendetta, and jealousy in the Church; he asks, "Whom are we going to evangelize if this is the way we act?" **(101).** We always seek to overcome evil with good (Rom 12:21). Francis advises, "Let us not allow ourselves to be robbed of the ideal of fraternal love!"

Other Ecclesial Challenges (102–109). (102). Laypersons are the majority of the Church; ordained ministers are necessarily at their service. The formation of the laity represents a significant pastoral challenge. **(103).** We need to create still broader opportunities for a more inclusive female presence in the Church, capitalizing on the "feminine genius." **(104).** Francis writes that the reservation of the priesthood to males "is not a question open to discussion"; efforts are better focused on seeking holiness and service. "A woman, Mary, is more important than the bishops." **(105).** Youth ministry needs renewal to respond better to current social changes; various youth associations and movements are truly the work of the Holy Spirit. **(106).** The task of evangelizing and educating the young is the duty of the entire community. **(107).** The dearth of vocations to the priesthood and religious life demands a deeper fervor in the entire Christian community; even in this situation the motivation of potential seminarians must be carefully scrutinized. **(108).** Francis affirms that he has not offered a complete diagnosis; the Church must continue to read "the signs of the times," listening to a wide variety of people. **(109).** Francis concludes this lengthy chapter with inspiring words: "Challenges exist to be overcome! Let us be realists, but without losing our joy, our boldness and our hope-filled commitment. Let us not allow ourselves to be robbed of missionary vigor!"

Chapter Three: The Proclamation of the Gospel

(**110**). Numerous challenges face the Church, yet we seek to promote authentic evangelization in the name of Jesus the Lord. This involves the joyful, patient, and progressive preaching of Jesus' death and resurrection. Jesus Christ is our absolute priority.

The Entire People of God Proclaims the Gospel. (**111**). Succinctly stated, the task of the Church is evangelization. **A People for Everyone (112–114)**. (**112**). God offers us salvation, clearly a work of mercy; no human effort can merit such a great gift. (**113**). No one is saved by oneself; salvation involves an interweaving of personal relationships within a human community. (**114**). The Church must be a place of mercy where all are welcomed, loved, forgiven, and encouraged.

A People of Many Faces (115–118). (**115**). Each people develops its culture with legitimate autonomy; each individual person is always situated in a culture. (**116**). Thus, Christianity does not simply have only one cultural expression; from her varied faces, the Church expresses its genuine catholicity. The Church integrates faith and culture through inculturation. (**117**). Properly understood, cultural diversity is not a threat to Church unity. The Church seeks to evangelize all cultures; she does not impose a specific cultural form around the world. (**118**). Faith and Church are to be expressed in legitimate forms appropriate for each culture; no single culture can exhaust the mystery of our redemption in Christ.

We Are All Missionary Disciples (119–121). (**119**). All the baptized, the totality of the faithful, are endowed with "an instinct of faith—*sensus fidei*—that helps them to discern what is truly of God." (**120**). Indeed, baptized persons are missionary disciples; "we no longer say that we are 'disciples' and 'missionaries,' but rather that we are always missionary disciples." (**121**). We are constantly being evangelized as well as actively engaged in our evangelizing mission.

The Evangelizing Power of Popular Piety (122–126).
(122). Culture and faith are intimately linked; often they are transmitted together. Thus, one may say that "a people continuously evangelizes itself." **(123).** Popular piety enables us to see how faith, once received, becomes embodied in culture and is constantly passed on. Pope Paul VI noted that "popular piety manifests a thirst for God": Pope Benedict XVI saw it as "a precious treasure of the Catholic Church." **(124).** Popular piety (popular spirituality, the people's mysticism) is truly a spirituality incarnated in the culture of the lowly and is a legitimate way of living the faith; it has a missionary power. **(125).** We approach it with the gaze of the Good Shepherd, who seeks not to judge but to love; it reflects the Holy Spirit active in people's hearts. **(126).** Expressions of popular piety have much to teach us; they are a *locus theologicus* [source of theology] that demands our attention.

Person to Person (127–129). **(127).** In our daily-life interactions, we bring the Gospel to the people we meet. **(128).** In Gospel communication, the first step is personal dialogue and personal witness. **(129).** The Gospel, communicated in categories proper to each culture, creates a new synthesis with that particular culture.

Charisms at the Service of a Communion That Evangelizes (130–131). **(130).** The Holy Spirit enriches the entire evangelizing Church with multiple charisms, making the Church more fruitful and effective in the world (e.g., for the promotion of peace). **(131).** The Holy Spirit alone can raise up diversity, plurality, and multiplicity while at the same time bringing about unity.

Culture, Thought, and Education (132–134). **(132).** Proclaiming the Gospel involves bringing it to professional, scientific, and academic circles. **(133).** Christians, theologians in particular, are to advance dialogue with the world of cultures and sciences. **(134).** Catholic educational facilities strive to join their work of education with explicit Gospel proclamation.

The Homily (135–136). (135). Preaching within the liturgy becomes a touchstone for judging a pastor's closeness to and ability to communicate with his people. **(136).** The Church needs renewed confidence in preaching, for through the preacher God is reaching out to people. **The Liturgical Context (137–138). (137).** Preaching within the liturgy is best seen as a dialogue between God and his people. **(138).** The homily is not a form of entertainment; it should be brief, not resembling a speech or a lecture nor upsetting the balance and rhythm of the liturgy.

A Mother's Conversation (139–141). (139). The Church is a mother; thus, preachers should preach in the same way a mother speaks to her child. **(140).** Like a mother, the preacher must manifest closeness to the people; his voice should be warm, unpretentious, and joyful. **(141).** As the Lord enjoyed talking with his people, the preacher should communicate the same enjoyment to his listeners.

Words That Set Hearts on Fire (142–144). (142). Heart-to-heart communication should mark the homily; concrete images further effective communication. **(143).** Inculturated preaching emerges from the heart; the task is to preach Jesus, not oneself. **(144).** To speak from the heart means that one's heart is both on fire and enlightened by the fullness of revelation. **Preparing to Preach. (145).** Preparation for preaching is so important a task that a prolonged time of study, prayer, reflection, and pastoral creativity must be devoted to it. A preacher who does not prepare is not "spiritual"; he is dishonest and irresponsible with the gifts he has received.

Reverence for Truth (146–148). (146). The preacher, after calling upon the Holy Spirit in prayer, focuses on the biblical text with true humility of heart; such preparation requires genuine love. **(147).** A depth understanding of the text is required to communicate its true message. Preaching should not be used to correct errors or to teach doctrine. **(148)**. A key point of biblical interpretation is to appreciate how a particular text is related to the Bible as a whole.

Personalizing the Word (149–151). (149). Personal familiarity with the Word of God is essential; the message of the readings will resonate deeply in people's hearts if it has first done so in the heart of their pastor. **(150)**. Today, people prefer to listen to witnesses; they thirst for authenticity; evangelizers are to speak of a God they personally know, as if they were seeing him. **(151)**. The preacher must be certain that God loves him, that Jesus Christ has saved him, and that his love always has the last word.

Spiritual Reading (152–153). (152). The practice of *lectio divina* (spiritual, prayerful reading of Scripture) is very helpful for preachers. **(153)**. A recollected reading of the text is also facilitated by asking personal questions of how the text applies to one's own life. **An Ear to the People (154–155). (154)**. The preacher needs to be close to the people to appreciate their reality; he needs a spiritual sensitivity for reading God's message in events; he practices "evangelical discernment." **(155)**. However, this does not mean talking about the latest news or a television program (though sometimes current events could be a "homily starter").

Homiletic Resources (156–159). (156). Preachers need to be trained for effective communication. **(157)**. Preaching is enhanced by appealing to images that are familiar to people, close to home, practical, and related to everyday life; it is said that a good homily should have an idea, a sentiment, and an image. **(158)**. Preachers need to be sensitive to their language, assuring that it truly communicates effectively. **(159)**. Priests, deacons, and laity are all enriched by gathering periodically to share homiletic resources and engage in communal faith sharing.

Evangelization and the Deeper Understanding of the *Kerygma* (160–162). **(160).** The Lord's missionary mandate includes the call to growth in faith; ongoing formation facilitates this maturation. **(161).** This call includes several elements: living the commandment of love, doctrinal appreciation, and living a moral life. **(162).** All this is preceded by God's gift of Baptism and the desire to give God glory.

Kerygmatic and Mystagogical Catechesis (163–168). **(163).** Education and catechesis, using Church resources, facilitate growth in faith. **(164).** The first proclamation must always be: Jesus loves you; he gave his life for you; he is always at your side. **(165).** All Christian formation consists in entering deeply into the Church's faith and teaching; this is enhanced by an evangelizer's attitudes of approachability, readiness for dialogue, patience, and a warm, nonjudgmental welcome. **(166).** The Church appreciates "mystagogic initiation," which includes progressive formation and a renewed appreciation of the liturgical signs of Christian initiation. **(167).** All catechesis should attend to the "way of beauty" (*via pulchritudinis*); beauty attracts, it inspires, it is an effective tool in transmitting the faith. **(168).** Evangelizers must not be "dour judges"; they should appear as joyful messengers of the good news and beauty of the Gospel.

Personal Accompaniment in Processes of Growth (169–173). **(169).** All evangelizers need to practice the "art of accompaniment," which facilitates closeness; it liberates and encourages growth in the Christian life. **(170).** Spiritual accompaniment seeks to lead others closer to God. **(171).** Experience facilitates better accompaniment; the art of listening is important. The best pedagogy is a gradual, step-by-step introduction to the faith. **(172).** The person accompanying will be patient and compassionate, not giving into frustrations and fears. **(173).** Genuine spiritual accompaniment also serves evangelization; "missionary disciples accompany missionary disciples." Note that Pope Francis proposes "accompaniment" as the model for youth ministry; see Chapter 7 of *Christus Vivit*, especially numbers 242–247.

Centered on the Word of God (174–175). (174). All evangelization is based on the Word of God, listened to, meditated upon, lived, celebrated, and witnessed to. **(175).** Study of Scripture, God's revealed word, is a door that must be opened to every believer.

CHAPTER FOUR: THE SOCIAL DIMENSION OF EVANGELIZATION

(176). Appreciating the integral nature of the mission of evangelization avoids accepting any partial or fragmentary approach, thus avoiding any impoverishment or distortion of authentic "integral evangelization." **Communal and Societal Repercussions of the Kerygma. (177).** The kerygma has a clear social content and has immediate moral implications centered on charity.

Confession of Faith and Commitment to Society (178–179). (178). Christ redeems not only the individual person, but the social relationships existing between people; he unties the knots of human affairs. There is a profound connection between evangelization and human advancement. **(179).** The Gospel is one of fraternity and justice; it demands practicing the mercy that God has shown us. We constantly affirm that the Church is missionary in her very identity.

The Kingdom and Its Challenge (180–181). (180). The Gospel is not merely about our personal relationship with God; it also seeks to portray the impact that the Gospel is to have on society and the building of Christ's Kingdom. **(181).** Evangelization is incomplete without manifesting the interplay between the Gospel and concrete human life, both personal and social.

The Church's Teaching on Social Questions (182–185). (182). Evangelization demands the integral promotion of each human person; practical implementation and the pursuit of the common good are essential. **(183).** Authentic faith involves a deep desire to change the world, to transmit values, to leave this world a better place than we found it; thus, "the Church cannot and must not remain on the sidelines in the fight for justice." **(184).** Truly, neither the pope nor the Church have a monopoly on the transformation of social realities; Christian communities must engage with the situation proper to their own country. **(185).** Two great issues face humanity today: first, the inclusion of the poor in society, and second, peace and social dialogue.

The Inclusion of the Poor in Society (186). Our faith in Christ who voluntarily became poor is the basis for our concern for society's most neglected members.

In Union with God, We Hear a Plea (187–192). (187). Every Christian and community is called to be an instrument of God for the liberation of the poor; our solidarity with the needy directly affects our relationship with God. **(188).** Following Jesus' command, we stand in solidarity with the poor, working to eliminate structural causes of poverty and promoting integral development. **(189).** The social function of property and the universal destination of goods are realities that come before private property. **(190).** Planet earth belongs to all of humanity. The more fortunate should voluntarily renounce some of their rights, placing their goods at the service of others; all need to grow in solidarity. **(191).** Christians with the help of their pastors are called to hear the cry of the poor; all are called to eliminate "the generalized practice of wastefulness." **(192).** We seek to promote education, health care, employment, and just wages for all.

Fidelity to the Gospel, Lest We Run in Vain (193–196).
(193). When we allow ourselves to be moved by the suffering
of others, we grow in mercy; we find joy when opportunities to
do a work of mercy open before us. **(194).** We avoid passivity,
dedicating ourselves to merciful, humble, and generous service of
the poor. **(195).** Unfortunately, a new self-centered paganism
is growing. **(196).** Limitless possibilities for consumption are
emerging, often making it difficult to offer the "gift of self" for
others' needs.

The Special Place of the Poor in God's People (197–201).
(197). The poor have a special place in God's heart; thus, he voluntarily became poor (2 Cor 8:9). Mary, a poor maiden, uttered her
"yes" to God, thus allowing salvation to come to us. **(198).** The
option for the poor is primarily a theological category, not a cultural,
sociological, or political one. Francis boldly asserts, "I want a Church
that is poor and for the poor." **(199).** Loving attention entails
appreciating the goodness of the poor, their life experience, their
culture, and their ways of living the faith. Without the preferential
option for the poor, the Gospel risks being misunderstood. **(200).**
The worst discrimination that the poor suffer is the lack of spiritual
care. **(201).** None of us can think we are exempt from concern for
the poor and for social justice.

The Economy and the Distribution of Income
(202–208). **(202).** Resolution of the structural causes of
poverty and inequality cannot be delayed; they are at the roots
of diverse social ills. **(203).** When voluntarily challenged by the
greater meaning of life, the vocation of business becomes a noble
vocation. **(204).** Humanity can no longer trust in unforeseen
market forces; specific initiatives geared to a better distribution of
income must be developed. **(205).** Francis pleads, "I beg the Lord
to grant us more politicians who are genuinely disturbed by the state

of society, the people, the lives of the poor!" **(206)**. Admittedly, enormous global problems exist; nations must cooperate to ensure the economic well-being of all countries, not just of a few. **(207)**. Church communities themselves must avoid drifting into "spiritual worldliness." **(208)**. Straightforwardly, Francis writes, "If anyone feels offended by my words, I would respond that I speak them with affection and with the best of intentions, quite apart from any personal interest or political ideology."

Concern for the Vulnerable (209–216). (209). Jesus, evangelizer par excellence, identifies especially with the little ones (cf. Mt 25:40). **(210)**. The Church, mother to all, must draw near to new forms of poverty and vulnerability: the homeless, the addicted, refugees, indigenous peoples, the elderly, and, in particular, migrants. **(211)**. Truly distressful is the emergence of various forms of human trafficking. **(212)**. Doubly poor are those women who endure exclusion, mistreatment, and violence, since they are frequently less able to defend their rights. **(213)**. The Church has particular love and concern for unborn children; this defense of unborn life is closely linked to the defense of all other human rights. **(214)**. Valuing every human person means that the Church cannot be expected to change her position on this question. **(215)**. Creation as a whole must be defended; Francis extensively quotes the Philippine bishops on ecological issues. **(216)**. Like Francis of Assisi, Christians must protect the fragile world in which we live.

The Common Good and Peace in Society (217–221). (217). We note that the Word of God speaks frequently about peace. **(218)**. When serious problems arise in society, the Church must raise her prophetic voice. **(219)**. Peace is much more than the absence of war; only a peace based on integral development will perdure. **(220)**. Christians must become involved, since "respon-

sible citizenship is a virtue, and participation in political life is a
moral obligation." **(221)**. Building peace, justice, and fraternity is
based on four principles, derived from the Church's social teaching.

Time Is Greater Than Space (222–225). **(222)**. Here one
finds the first principle for progress in building up people. **(223)**.
This principle enables us to work slowly, but surely, without being
obsessed with immediate results. **(224)**. Our focus is in-depth
people-building; the goal is not obtaining immediate results or
short-term political gains. **(225)**. Thus, in evangelization we
emphasize suitable processes and concerns for the long run.

Unity Prevails over Conflict (226–230). **(226)**. Conflicts
cannot be ignored or concealed; they are faced, so that we do not lose
our perspective and sense of the profound unity of reality. **(227)**.
It is best to face conflicts directly, resolve them, and learn from
them. "Blessed are the peacemakers" (Mt 5:9). **(228)**. The goal is
the building of friendship in society, preserving the best from all
sides. **(229)**. This Gospel-based principle recalls that Christ made
peace through the blood of his cross (see Col 1:20). **(230)**. We
appreciate that the Spirit can harmonize every diversity, resulting
in a "reconciled diversity."

Realities Are More Important Than Ideas (231–233). **(231)**.
We engage in a continuous dialogue between ideas and realities,
aware that it is dangerous to dwell in the realm of words
alone. **(232)**. Ideas and conceptual elaborations are at the service
of communication, understanding, and praxis. **(233)**. In reality, we
seek to have words become flesh; this is essential to evangelization.
We perform works of justice, achieving beneficial charitable works,
avoiding fruitless Gnosticism.

The Whole Is Greater Than the Part (234–237). **(234)**.
An innate tension exists between globalization and localization;
we appreciate both and thus avoid either extreme. **(235)**. The

whole is greater than just the sum of the parts; we seek to broaden our horizons while continuing to work in our local neighborhood. **(236)**. We promote the convergence of diverse people and the growth of the common good. **(237)**. In Christianity, we appreciate that each people receives in its own way the fullness of the Gospel and embodies it in prayer, fraternity, justice, and celebration.

Social Dialogue as a Contribution to Peace (238–241). **(238)**. Evangelization involves the path of dialogue with society, with cultures and the sciences, and with other believers. **(239)**. The Church, proclaiming the Gospel of peace, wishes to cooperate with all national and international bodies to build consensus and establish an inclusive society. **(240)**. The State has the responsibility of safeguarding the common good; it needs to be committed to political dialogue and consensus building. All this requires "profound social humility." **(241)**. Admittedly, "the Church does not have solutions for every particular issue"; she always promotes the fundamental value of human life in all political activity.

Dialogue between Faith, Reason, and Science (242–243). **(242)**. Dialogue between science and faith enters into the work of evangelization at the service of peace. The Church employs methods proper to the empirical sciences and integrates them within her faith perspective. **(243)**. The Church does not wish to hold back the progress of science; faith does not contradict science.

Ecumenical Dialogue (244–246). **(244)**. The credibility of the Christian message would be much greater if Christians overcame their divisions. **(245)**. Ecumenical participation at the 2012 Synod of Bishops was a true gift from God and a precious Christian witness. **(246)**. Divided Christianity is a scandal; it negatively affects the preaching of the Gospel.

Relations with Judaism (247–249). **(247)**. The Catholic Church has a special regard for the Jewish people; they believe in the one God with whom they have a covenant and they accept his revealed word. **(248)**. Dialogue and friendship with the children of Israel are part of the life of Jesus' disciples. **(249)**. God continues to work among his people of the Old Covenant today.

Interreligious Dialogue (250–254). (250). Interreligious or interfaith dialogue is a necessary condition for world peace. **(251)**. Authentic openness involves both fidelity to one's own faith while appreciating the values of the other; indeed, dialogue enriches both sides. Evangelization and dialogue actually support and nourish one another. **(252)**. One finds an impressive list of communalities between Islam and Christianity; examples are: faith in the one God, necessity of prayer, reverence for Mary the mother of Jesus. **(253)**. Mutual respect is needed for dialogue to prosper; collaboration for world peace can be an important mutual commitment. **(254)**. God's salvation is open to all people through association with the Paschal Mystery (see *Gaudium et Spes* 22).

Social Dialogue in a Context of Religious Freedom (255–258). (255). Religious freedom is a fundamental human right; the Church promotes a healthy pluralism, tolerance, and peace. **(256)**. Unfortunately, sometimes journalists have a superficial understanding of religion; some politicians seek to use religion for their political advantage. **(257)**. As believers, we also feel close to those who follow no religious tradition. **(258)**. In all circumstances, we seek to demonstrate the social dimension of the Gospel by our words, attitudes, and deeds.

Chapter Five: Spirit-Filled Evangelizers

259–261. (259). Spirit-filled evangelizers are fearlessly open to the workings of the Holy Spirit; they act with boldness (*parrhesia*); they manifest a life transfigured by God's presence. **(260)**. The pope does not intend to present a complete synthesis of Christian spirituality; he is offering some insights about the spirit of the new evangelization. **(261).** Francis implores the Holy Spirit to stir up enthusiasm for a new chapter of evangelization "full of fervor, joy, generosity, courage, boundless love, and attraction!"

Reasons for a Renewed Missionary Impulse (262–263). **(262).** Spirit-filled evangelizers pray and work. Mystical notions without a solid social and missionary outreach do not help evangelization; the same is true for a privatized and individualistic spirituality. **(263).** Every period of history is unique. The challenges today are not harder; they are simply different.

Personal Encounter with the Saving Love of Jesus (264–267). **(264).** The primary reason for evangelizing is the love of Jesus; this can be experienced by simply standing before a crucifix or before the Blessed Sacrament. In everything we need to recover a contemplative spirit. **(265).** Jesus' whole life is precious. We always remember that the Gospel responds to our deepest needs; we are offered his personal friendship. This is the source of missionary enthusiasm. **(266).** A true missionary remains a disciple; he senses that Jesus is alive with him in his missionary undertakings. **(267).** In union with Jesus, we seek and love what he seeks and loves. We always evangelize for the greater glory of the Father who loves us.

The Spiritual Savor of Being a People (268–274). **(268).** Poignantly stated, "Mission is at once a passion for Jesus and a passion for his people." **(269).** Jesus himself is the model of missionary evangelization; this is seen in his evident sensitivity to people. **(270).** Jesus wants us to touch human misery, the suffering flesh of others; in this experience we will know "the power of tenderness." **(271).** As we engage the world, we give convincing reasons for our hope, always with courtesy, respect, and a clear conscience (1 Pet 3:15–16), seeking to light a fire in the heart of the world. **(272).** Francis asserts, "If we want to advance in the spiritual life, then, we must constantly be missionaries." **(273).** Each of us must believe, "I am a mission on this earth; that is the reason why I am here in this world." **(274)**. As evangelizers we must exude "God's infinite tenderness!"

The Mysterious Working of the Risen Christ and His Spirit (275–280). **(275)**. Our faith assures us, "Jesus Christ truly lives" (*Christus Vivit*). Christ, risen and glorified, is the wellspring of our hope. **(276)**. Christ's resurrection is a present event containing a vital power; all who evangelize are instruments of that power. **(277)**. Even in difficult circumstances, the most powerful message that evangelizers can offer the world is that of Christ's resurrection. **(278)**. Faith means believing in God who never abandons us and that he can bring good out of difficulties—even evil. **(279)**. God is able to act in every situation; often his fruitfulness is invisible. We always rest in the tenderness of the arms of the Father. **(280)**. Keeping our missionary fervor alive calls for trust in the Holy Spirit, who "helps us in our weakness" (Rom 8:26); he knows what is needed in every time and place.

The Missionary Power of Intercessory Prayer (281–283). **(281)**. The prayer of intercession moves us to take up the task of evangelization and to seek the good of others. **(282)**. When evangelizers rise from prayer, their hearts are more open; they are freed from self-absorption and become desirous of doing good and sharing their lives with others. **(283)**. Great saints were great intercessors. Intercession is like a "leaven" in God's heart; the result is that his power, his love, and his faithfulness are more clearly manifest in the midst of the people.

Mary, Mother of Evangelization. **(284)**. Mary is Mother of the Church that evangelizes; with her we better understand the spirit of evangelization. **Jesus' Gift to His People (285–286)**. **(285)**. Jesus felt the consoling presence of his mother and friend on Calvary; he left us his mother to be our mother. The Lord did not wish to leave the Church without this "icon of womanhood." **(286)**. Mary transformed a stable into a home; she is the humble handmaid who sings God's praises; with her pierced heart she understands all our pain, offering her maternal, loving comfort. Mary is "a sign of hope for all peoples suffering the birth pangs of justice."

Star of the New Evangelization (287–288). (287). Today we look to Mary to enable new disciples to become evangelizers. Her "exceptional pilgrimage of faith represents a constant point of reference for the Church." **(288).** There is a Marian "style" to the Church's work of evangelization, reflecting the revolutionary nature of love and tenderness. She recognizes the traces of God's Spirit in events great and small. Finally, Francis concludes with a six-paragraph prayer to Mary, Star of the New Evangelization.

3

Misericordiae Vultus
The Face of Mercy

(April 11, 2015)

This rather brief document is a papal "bull," a kind of official letter or declaration; here Pope Francis convokes an Extraordinary Jubilee of Mercy to commemorate the fiftieth anniversary of the close of the Second Vatican Council in 1965. Francis asserts that the Church "feels a great need to keep this event alive" because with the Council "the Church entered a new phase of her history" (4). The theme of "mercy" emerges from the Council itself; in his opening speech at Vatican II, Pope John XXIII, now a canonized saint, said that the Church wished "to use the medicine of mercy" as she sought to evangelize the modern world. Francis has incorporated the theme of mercy into his papal motto, *Miserando atque eligendo* (Chosen through mercy).

Misericordiae Vultus comprises twenty-five numbered sections, highlighting numerous creative insights into the virtue of mercy. "We need constantly to contemplate the mystery of mercy; it is a wellspring of joy, serenity, and peace" (2). "It is proper to God to exercise mercy" (6). "Everything in him [Jesus] speaks of mercy. Nothing in him is devoid of compassion" (8). "Wherever there are Christians, everyone should find an oasis of mercy" (12). "Everyone, in fact, without exception, is called to embrace the call to mercy"

(18). Jesus reveals "the great gift of mercy" that is "a source of new life" (20). Mary's "entire life was patterned after the presence of mercy made flesh" (24). "The Church is called above all to be a credible witness to mercy" (25).

During the Jubilee Year of Mercy—and always—Christians are challenged by Pope Francis to deeply integrate mercy into their lives. Some guidelines may help our daily "living-in-mercy": (1) Manifesting God's mercy is a duty for every Christian; it is not optional. (2) Mercy addresses suffering and "poverty" of various types in today's world: physical, spiritual, personal, structural, psychological, and so on. Francis calls Christians to practice the corporal and spiritual works of mercy (15). (3) "Let us enter more deeply into the heart of the Gospel where the poor have a special experience of God's mercy" (15). (4) Mercy is not easy; its demands are often inconvenient and unpredictable; it impinges on our personal plans and schedules. We cannot calculate when mercy will be demanded of us. (5) Let us be motivated by the Beatitudes, especially Jesus' words: "Blessed are the merciful, for they shall obtain mercy" (Mt 5:7).

Misericordiae Vultus
Synthesis Text

LETTER FOR THE JUBILEE OF MERCY

Centrality of Mercy (1–2). (1). Jesus Christ is the face of the Father's mercy; these words capture the mystery of the Christian faith. By his words and actions, indeed, in his entire person, Jesus reveals the mercy of God. **(2).** We need to constantly contemplate this mystery of mercy; it is a wellspring of joy, serenity, and peace; it is the source of our salvation. Mercy is the bridge that connects God and people, opening hearts to being loved forever—despite our sinfulness.

Jubilee of Mercy (3–5). (3). We are invited to gaze attentively on mercy, so we may become more effective signs of the Father's action in our lives; this is the motive for having an *Extraordinary Jubilee of Mercy*. The year opens on December 8, 2015, the Solemnity of the Immaculate Conception, a feast revealing God's saving mercy. Holy Doors will be open in every diocese for the entire year. **(4).** This date commemorates the fiftieth anniversary of the closing of the Second Vatican Council in 1965. The Church "feels a great need to keep this event alive," since it was the beginning of a new phase of evangelization. Called by Saint John XXIII, the Council wished to show the Church as a loving, compassionate, and merciful mother to all. It is noteworthy that the annual feast day of John XXIII is October 11, commemorating the opening day of Vatican II on October 11, 1962. **(5).** The Jubilee Year closes on the Feast of Christ the King, emphasizing Christ's Lordship and his merciful love for all peoples of the world.

Our Merciful God (6–7). (6). Thomas Aquinas asserted, "It is proper to God to exercise mercy." These words show that God's mercy, rather than a sign of weakness, is the mark of his omnipotence. The Old Testament frequently connects the words "patient" and "merciful"; God lifts up those who are bowed down. The Psalmist says, "He heals the brokenhearted and binds up their wounds" (Ps 147:3). **(7).** In Psalm 136 the words "For his mercy endures forever" are repeated after each verse. Before his passion, Jesus prayed with this psalm of mercy.

Jesus, Mercy Incarnate (8–9). (8). Affirming God's mercy, John the Evangelist asserts, "God is love" (1 Jn 4:8, 16). This merciful love is made visible and tangible in Jesus' entire life. All the signs he works for sinners, the poor, marginalized, sick, and suffering are meant to teach mercy. "Everything in him speaks of mercy. Nothing in him is devoid of compassion." The call of Matthew (Mt 9:9–13) is narrated within the context of mercy. Saint Bede the Venerable comments on Matthew's calling, noting that Jesus looked at Matthew with merciful love and chose him: *miserando atque eligendo.* Pope Francis writes, "This expression impressed me so much that I chose it for my episcopal motto." **(9).** Jesus told several parables devoted to mercy: the lost sheep, the lost coin, and the father with two sons (Lk 15:1–32). Mercy must also include forgiveness, up to seventy times seven times (Mt 18:22). Jesus declares, "Blessed are the merciful, for they shall obtain mercy" (Mt 5:7).

Mercy and Church Life (10–12). (10). "Mercy is the very foundation of the Church's life. All of her pastoral activity should be caught up in the tenderness she makes present to believers.... The Church's very credibility is seen in how she shows merciful and compassionate love." Since the practice of mercy is waning in the wider culture, now is the time for the Church to take up once again the joyful call to mercy. **(11).** We have much to learn from Saint John Paul II's encyclical *Dives in Misericordia.* We can capitalize on the fact that many in the Church and world today, guided by a lively sense of faith, are turning almost spontaneously to the mercy of God. **(12).** The Church is tasked to announce the mercy of God, "the beating heart of the Gospel." Wherever the Church is present (parishes, communities, associations, movements), "wherever there are Christians, everyone should find an oasis of mercy."

Living the Jubilee Year of Mercy (13–14). (13). We want to live the Jubilee Year in light of the Lord's words: *Merciful like the Father.* The Word of God, the Scriptures, will help dispose us to be capable of mercy. **(14).** The practice of *pilgrimage* has a special place in a Holy Year; this can be practiced by going to the Holy Door in our dioceses. We are also to make a pilgrimage in our faith, seeking to avoid hard judgments, eliminating all gossip, accepting the good in every person, and practicing forgiveness. Daily we are to compassionately practice the "motto" of the Holy Year: *Merciful like the Father.*

Enfleshing the Challenge of Mercy (15–16). (15). During the Holy Year we seek to open our hearts to those living on the outermost fringes of society; their voices are often "drowned out by the indifference of the rich." Let us open our eyes and see the misery of the world and the wounds of our brothers and sisters; let them "feel the warmth of our presence, our friendship, and our fraternity." We can concretize our faith by practicing the corporal and spiritual works of mercy, recalling the criteria upon which we will be judged (Mt 25:31–45). Christ himself is present and visible in the flesh of the tortured, crushed, scourged, malnourished, and exiled; we must touch them! **(16).** We both proclaim and live this year of the Lord's favor, his mercy. And, when we do acts of mercy, let us always do them with cheerfulness (Rom 12:8).

Season of Mercy (17–18). (17). During this Jubilee Year, the season of Lent should be lived more intensely, with more authentic prayer, fasting, and works of charity. The words of the prophets can guide us in our Lenten pilgrimage (Mic 7:18–19; Isa 58:6–11). The initiative of "24 hours for the Lord" invites a return to the Sacrament of Reconciliation. Confessors must be authentic signs of the Father's mercy, since they participate in the very mission of Jesus. They are called to embrace the repentant son; they are to be "a sign of the primacy of mercy always, everywhere, and in every situation, no matter what." **(18).** The pope will send out *Missionaries of Mercy* to be living signs of the Father's readiness to welcome those in search of his pardon and mercy. Worldwide, bishops should welcome these preachers of mercy, as they call the faithful "to the throne of grace, that we may receive mercy and find grace" (Heb 4:16).

A Universal Message (19). No one should be indifferent to the call to experience mercy. Specifically mentioned are "men and women belonging to criminal organizations of any kind" and those who think that "life depends on money." The same invitation extends to those who "either perpetuate or participate in corruption," which is a "festering wound" and a "grave sin that cries to heaven for vengeance." Corruption is a "hardening of the heart" and "a work of darkness" that can end up destroying our very human existence. Indeed, this Jubilee Year is an opportune moment to change our lives, "a special time of mercy offered by the Church."

Mercy and Justice (20–21). (20). Justice and mercy are two dimensions of the single reality of the fullness of love. Jesus is constantly revealing the great gift of mercy. When questioned why he ate with tax collectors and sinners, he replied, "Go and learn the meaning of 'I desire mercy not sacrifice'" (Mt 9:13). Jesus' response reflects words from the prophet Hosea: "I desire love and not sacrifice" (Hos 6:6). Saint Paul also affirms that God's justice is his mercy. **(21).** Mercy is not opposed to justice; rather, it expresses God's way of reaching out to sinners. Again, Hosea shows how God, angry with his unfaithful people, relents in his planned punishment: "My compassion grows warm and tender…, I will not again destroy Ephraim; for I am God and not man" (Hos 11:8–9). Saint Augustine in a homily says, "It is easier for God to hold back anger than mercy." While it is true that God moves beyond justice with his mercy and forgiveness, this does not mean that justice should be devalued or rendered superfluous.

Receiving and Living Mercy (22–23). (22). A Jubilee Year involves granting indulgences, a sharing in God's unbounded forgiveness. It is through the Paschal Mystery and the mediation of the Church that reconciliation with God is made possible. The sacraments of Reconciliation and the Eucharist extend the Father's mercy to the entire life of the believer. **(23).** An aspect of mercy extends beyond the confines of the Church; it relates us to Judaism and Islam. Both of these faiths consider mercy to be one of God's most important attributes. It is hoped that the year of mercy will foster "an encounter with these religions and with other noble religious traditions," eliminating every form of closed-mindedness, disrespect, violence, and discrimination.

Mother of Mercy (24). No one has penetrated the profound mystery of the incarnation like Mary. "Her entire life was patterned after the presence of mercy made flesh." She sings God's praises because he extends his mercy from generation to generation (Lk 1:50). At the foot of the cross, she and John the disciple witnessed the words of forgiveness spoken by Jesus. "This supreme expression of mercy toward those who crucified him shows us the point to which the mercy of God can reach." In the *Salve Regina*, Mary is called *Mater Misericordiae* (Mother of Mercy). There are many saints of mercy, especially the apostle of mercy, Saint Faustina Kowalska.

Proclaiming and Witnessing God's Mercy (25). In the Jubilee Year and always, the Church feels the urgent need to proclaim God's mercy; her life is authentic and credible only when she becomes a convincing herald of mercy. Because God's mercy never ends, the Church must constantly be a credible witness to mercy; God's boundless mercy must well up and overflow in her unceasingly like a great river. The Church must be a convincing sign of God's compassion and comfort. "May she never tire of extending mercy!"

[NOTE: *Misericordiae Vultus* is dated April 11, 2015, the Second Sunday of Easter, popularly known as Divine Mercy Sunday. The section headings used here are not found in the original text; they are supplied by the editor of this synthesis presentation.]

4

Laudato Sí
On Care for Our Common Home

(May 24, 2015)

Pope Francis has written a lengthy encyclical that is entirely focused on the environment. This 183-page document proposes that the care of the earth is a moral and spiritual concern; it goes beyond simple matters of science, economics, and politics. Boldly, Pope Francis argues that the environment is in crisis; this has serious consequences, especially for the poor. Thus, Francis issues an urgent call to action, involving both immediate and long-range goals. He pointedly asks, "What kind of world do we want to leave to those who come after us, to children who are now growing up?" (LS 160). The document opens with a quote from the canticle of Saint Francis of Assisi; all this material will certainly become an important addition to Catholic Social Teaching begun by Pope Leo XIII's *Rerum Novarum* in 1891.

Francis seeks to "address every person living on this planet.... I would like to enter into dialogue with all people about our common home" (3). Given his universal audience, Francis quotes an immense range of resources, such as former popes, various saints, a Sufi mystic, and numerous secular sources. After describing the realities of environmental degradation, Francis asserts that religions can make a rich contribution to the debate. Francis invites us to adopt "the gaze of Jesus" (96–100). An honest evaluation notes the human roots of the ecological crisis; an "integral ecology" is urgently needed. Concrete lines of approach and action are identified. Finally, Francis explores the topic of ecological education and spirituality, appealing to individuals, families, communities, and all nations to actively seek to make a difference through concrete, tangible initiatives.

Risking oversimplification, one can identify various elements of a response to *Laudato Sí*. We must take to heart the fact that care for God's creation and our common home is an urgent moral and spiritual challenge. Our sensitivity to the present crisis demands a deeper appreciation of how the poor are severely impacted; our solidarity with all members of the human family must deepen. Further technological and economic development must truly serve all human beings and advance their dignity, especially the vulnerable (e.g., unborn children, people with disabilities, and victims of human trafficking). We seek to act now, retaining our hope and joy as we live out a vision of renewed relationships with God, ourselves, one another, and all creation.

Laudato Sí
Synthesis Text

INTRODUCTION

(1). *"Laudato Sí, Mí Signore"*— *"Praise Be to You, My Lord."* In these words of his beautiful canticle, Saint Francis of Assisi reminds us that our common home, the earth, is like a sister and mother to us. (2). This sister now cries out because of the harm inflicted upon her due to the irresponsible use and abuse of her resources. Symptoms of this sickness are evident in the soil, water, air, and all forms of life.

Nothing in This World Is Indifferent to Us (3–6). (3). In 1963, Pope John XXIII wrote *Pacem in Terris* as the world teetered on the brink of nuclear crisis. Today, in the light of global environmental deterioration, Pope Francis seeks dialogue with all people about our common home. **(4).** In 1971, Pope Paul VI spoke of ecological concern as a "tragic consequence" of unchecked human activity, highlighting the urgent need for radical change in the conduct of humanity. **(5).** Pope John Paul II called for a global ecological conversion and an authentic human ecology, noting that all human development has a moral character. **(6).** Pope Benedict XVI observed that "the book of nature is one and indivisible," including the environment, life, sexuality, the family, social relations, and other dimensions.

United by the Same Concern (7–9). (7). These papal statements echo the reflections of numerous scientists, philosophers, theologians, and civic groups, including the beloved Ecumenical Patriarch Bartholomew. **(8).** The patriarch has emphasized the need for repentance due to the "ecological damage" we have caused; he asserts that "to commit a crime against the natural world is a sin against ourselves and a sin against God." **(9).** Bartholomew speaks of the ethical and spiritual roots of environmental problems, asking that we replace "consumption with sacrifice, greed with generosity, wastefulness with a spirit of sharing."

Saint Francis of Assisi (10–12). (10). Pope Francis says that he does not wish to write this encyclical without recalling the attractive and compelling figure of Francis of Assisi, his guide and inspiration as pope. This Assisi saint is an example of care for both the vulnerable and the earth. **(11).** Saint Francis helps everyone to see the importance of an "integral ecology"; he communed with all of nature, calling all creatures by the name of brother or sister. **(12).** Francis, faithful to Scripture, sees nature as a magnificent book in which God speaks and enables us through analogy to know the person of the creator (cf. Wis 13:5). "The world is a joyful mystery to be contemplated with gladness and praise."

My Appeal (13–16). (13). Pope Francis has enunciated an "urgent challenge to protect our common home," to collaborate in building the home we all share. **(14).** Francis appeals for a new dialogue about how we are shaping the future of the planet. This requires a new and universal solidarity. **(15).** This encyclical seeks to add to the Church's social teaching; it has five points: (1) review of the present ecological crisis; (2) Judeo-Christian principles; (3) the deepest causes of the present crisis; (4) proposals for dialogue and action; and (5) guidelines for human development. **(16).** Other pivotal questions will be examined, such as the intimate relationship between the poor and the fragility of the planet, paradigms and forms of power, the throwaway culture, and the proposal of a new lifestyle.

CHAPTER ONE: WHAT IS HAPPENING TO OUR COMMON HOME?

(17). A fresh analysis of our present situation is needed, examining what is happening to the earth, "our common home." **(18).** Humanity is experiencing a more intensified pace of life and work, which might be called "rapidification." The goals of this reality are not necessarily geared to the common good and sustainable human development. **(19).** We are called to review the questions troubling us today and to become personally involved in what is happening to our world.

I. Pollution and Climate Change: Pollution, Waste, and the Throwaway Culture (20–22). (20). Some forms of pollution are part of everyone's daily experience; concrete examples abound. Sometimes one solution results in creating other problems. **(21).** Francis forcefully asserts, "The earth, our home, is beginning to look more and more like an immense pile of filth." **(22).** Many current problems are closely linked to a throwaway culture. We have not yet developed a circular model of recycling and production.

Climate as a Common Good (23–26). (23). The climate belongs to all and is meant for all; it is a common good. Numerous scientific studies indicate that the increase in greenhouse gases is mainly the result of human activity. **(24).** If present trends continue, this century may well witness extraordinary climate change and an unprecedented destruction of ecosystems. **(25).** The global problem of climate change represents one of the principal challenges facing humanity today. Environmental degradation results in significant human problems (e.g., poverty, lack of food, forced migration, etc.). **(26).** Urgent progress is needed to control the emission of various polluting gases, to develop sources of renewable energy, to develop storage technologies, and to improve energy efficiency in a variety of ways.

II. The Issue of Water (27–31). (27). Clearly, it is not possible to sustain the present level of consumption in developed countries. **(28).** Fresh drinking water, indispensable for human life, is an issue of primary importance, especially in places like Africa. **(29).** A serious problem is the quality of water available to the poor; unsafe water results in many deaths and the spread of water-related diseases. **(30).** Access to safe, drinkable water is a basic and universal human right; this is often denied to the poor. **(31).** Water scarcity results in numerous related problems (e.g., the cost of food and other products).

III. Loss of Biodiversity (32–42). (32). Shortsighted approaches to the economy, commerce, and production result in the plundering of the earth's resources. **(33).** Many valuable species become extinct due to human activity. **(34).** Even invisible species (microorganisms) are critical to maintaining the ecological equilibrium. **(35).** Alternative approaches that protect biodiversity must be explored. **(36)**. Caring for ecosystems demands farsightedness. **(37)**. Thankfully, some countries have made ecological progress. **(38)**. Our planet has some "richly biodiverse lungs," such as the Amazon and Congo basins. **(39)**. Virgin forests, wetlands, and mangrove swamps need protection, not replacement. **(40)**. The world's waters are an essential source of our food supply. **(41)**. Destroyed coral reefs become "underwater cemeteries bereft of color and life." **(42)**. Additional resources are needed to more fully understand how ecosystems function and impact the environment.

IV. Decline in the Quality of Human Life and the Breakdown of Society (43–47). **(43)**. We need to consider the effects on human life of environmental deterioration, development models, and the throwaway culture. **(44)**. The unruly growth of cities brings many problems and urban chaos. **(45)**. The privatization of certain spaces often limits people's access to places of beauty and relaxation. **(46)**. There are clear social dimensions to global change; numerous negative impacts are apparent. **(47)**. In addition, "when media and the digital world become omnipresent, their influence can stop people from learning how to live wisely, to think deeply, and to love generously."

V. Global Inequality (48–52). **(48)**. The human environment and the natural environment deteriorate together; often the poor suffer the most. **(49)**. A true ecological approach *always* becomes a social approach; thus, we are able to hear *both the cry of the earth and the cry of the poor*. **(50)**. Some assert that solving the problems of the poor means a reduction in the birth rate; the real problem lies with "extreme and selective consumerism" on the part of some. It is alarming that approximately a third of all food produced is discarded. **(51)**. An "ecological debt" exists, particularly between the global north and south; some examples are the mercury pollution in gold mining and the export of waste materials to developing countries. **(52).** The foreign debt of poor countries has become a way of controlling them. We need to strengthen the conviction that we are one single human family; we must address the "globalization of indifference."

VI. Weak Responses (53–59). (53). Situations today have caused sister earth to cry out; never have we so mistreated our common home as we have in the last two hundred years. **(54).** International political responses to the ecological crisis have been very weak; economic interests appear to have the upper hand. **(55).** While some people and countries have a growing ecological sensitivity, this has not changed their harmful habits of consumption. **(56).** Clearly, environmental degradation and human and ethical deterioration are closely linked. **(57).** The depletion of certain resources may result in future wars. **(58).** Despite our failures, gestures of generosity, solidarity, and care well up within us, since we were made for love. **(59).** We must be alert to various false or superficial ecological approaches that promote complacency and evasiveness.

VII. A Variety of Opinions (60–61). (60). Various viable scenarios need to be generated, since there is no one path to a solution. **(61).** The Church has no reason to offer a definite opinion; everyone needs to take "a frank look at the facts to see that our common home is falling into serious disrepair." Indeed, "we immediately see that humanity has disappointed God's expectations."

CHAPTER TWO: THE GOSPEL OF CREATION

(62). This document is addressed to all people of goodwill, yet it offers a chapter on the convictions of believers. Why? Religions can make a rich contribution toward an integral ecology.

I. The Light Offered by Faith (63–64). (63). The ecological crisis is very complex; thus, solutions are not to be found in only one way of interpreting and transforming reality. Various peoples and cultures have riches to contribute. **(64).** Francis seeks to show how faith convictions can offer Christians and other believers ample motivation to care for nature.

II. The Wisdom of the Biblical Accounts (65–75). (65). In the theology of creation, all God's creation is *very good* (Gen 1:31), and humans have an infinite dignity, since they are created out of love and made in God's image and likeness (Gen 1:26). **(66).** Human life is grounded in three fundamental and closely inter-twined relationships: with God, our neighbor, and the earth itself; these connections are ruptured by sin. **(67).** We are not God! Yet, humanity is given "dominion" over the earth (see Gen 1:28), not to exploit it, but to keep and till this garden that belongs to God. **(68).** This responsibility for God's earth demands that human beings must respect the laws of nature and the delicate equilibria existing between creatures. **(69).** We are called to recognize that all other living beings have a value of their own in God's eyes.

(70). The biblical stories of Cain and Abel and of Noah emphasize that we must respect our relationship with ourselves, with others, with God, and with the earth. **(71).** Through the one good man, Noah, God opened a path of salvation. The Creator also mandated the seventh day as a day of rest, a *Sabboth*, as well as the Jubilee Year after every forty-nine years. **(72).** The Psalms exhort us to praise God and live our lives with him and beside him. **(73).** As seen in the writings of the prophets, the God who liberates and saves is the same God who created the universe. **(74).** The experiences of the Babylonian captivity and, centuries later, the Roman persecution manifest that "injustice is not invincible." **(75).** If one forgets that God is all-powerful and is the Creator, one then usually ends up worshipping earthly powers and usurping the place of God.

III. The Mystery of the Universe (76–83). **(76).** In the Judeo-Christian tradition, the word "creation" broadly includes "God's loving plan in which every creature has its own value and significance." **(77).** The universe did not emerge arbitrarily; creation results from God's love. Basil the Great described the Creator as "goodness without measure." **(78).** While admiring the grandeur and immensity of nature, we must also practice human responsibility toward it. This also demands leaving behind "the modern myth of unlimited material progress." **(79).** In human history, freedom, growth, salvation, and love can blossom or may lead to decadence and destruction.

(80). Yet God can also bring good out of the evil humans have done. The Holy Spirit "knows how to loosen the knots of human affairs, including the most complex and inscrutable." **(81).** The emergence of a personal being (humans) within a material universe presupposes the direct action of God. **(82).** Attitudes such as "profit and gain," "might is right," and "winner takes all" are clearly at odds with the ideals of harmony, justice, fraternity, and peace proposed by Jesus. **(83).** The ultimate destiny of the universe is *not* in us; it is in the risen Christ who illumines all things, leading them back to their Creator.

IV. The Message of Each Creature in the Harmony of Creation (84–88). **(84).** The entire material universe speaks of God's love; everything is "a caress of God." **(85).** God has written a precious book; for believers to contemplate creation is to hear God's message and to live in love and hope. **(86).** The whole universe shows forth the inexhaustible riches of God. The Church's *Catechism* teaches, "God wills the *interdependence of creatures.*" **(87).** When our vision sees God reflected in all that exists, we are moved to praise the Lord. This sentiment is captured in the hymn of Saint Francis of Assisi, where he speaks of Brother Sun, Sister Moon, Brother Wind, Sister Water, and Brother Fire. **(88).** Nature manifests God and is also a locus of his presence; discovering this presence leads us to cultivate the "ecological virtues."

V. A Universal Communion (89–92). (89). God has joined us closely to the world around us; thus, we feel the pain of desertification and the extinction of species. **(90).** However, not all living beings are on the same level; for example, we do not divinize the earth. We defend all creatures, but human life has a clear preeminence. **(91).** Our communion with nature cannot be real "if our hearts lack tenderness, compassion, and concern for our fellow human beings," the poor in particular. **(92).** Our sense of fraternity excludes nothing and no one; as brothers and sisters we are on a wonderful pilgrimage together.

VI. The Common Destination of Goods (93–95). (93). Whether one is a believer or not, all agree today that the earth is a shared inheritance; thus, every ecological approach must incorporate a social perspective. The Church defends the legitimate right to private property, but this right is not absolute, due to mitigating factors. **(94).** The rich and the poor have equal dignity; all deserve equal access to a dignified human life. **(95).** The natural environment, a collective good, is the patrimony of all humanity and the responsibility of everyone.

VII. The Gaze of Jesus (96–100). (96). Jesus invited his disciples to recognize God as Father and his paternal relationship with all his creatures (cf. Lk 12:6; Mt 6:26). **(97).** The Lord was in constant touch with nature, inviting others to appreciate its beauty. **(98).** Jesus amazed others by living in full harmony with creation; he sanctified human labor, asserting that in this way humans collaborate with God for the redemption of humanity. **(99).** The destiny of all creation is bound up with the mystery of Christ's incarnation through which the Word "became flesh" (Jn 1:14). **(100).**

Our incarnational faith leads us to direct our gaze to the end of time when all reality will be imbued with the radiant presence of the risen One.

CHAPTER THREE: THE HUMAN ROOTS OF THE ECOLOGICAL CRISIS

(101). We now turn our attention to the human origins of the ecological crisis and the current dominant technocratic paradigm of human activity.

I. Technology: Creativity and Power (102–105). (102). Humanity has entered a new era, a crossroads, after two centuries of enormous waves of change. We rejoice in numerous human advances, wonderful products of God-given human creativity. **(103).** Technoscience, when well directed, can produce important improvements in the quality of human life. **(104).** Humanity has achieved impressive power over itself, yet "nothing ensures that it will be used wisely." One immediately thinks of "the increasingly deadly arsenal of weapons available for modern warfare." **(105).** Every increase in power is *not* automatically an increase in human responsibility, values, and a sensitive conscience.

II. The Globalization of the Technocratic Paradigm (106–114). (106). An undifferentiated and one-dimensional paradigm of development that foresees unlimited growth attracts many proponents; however, it is a "false notion" since it is based on "the lie that there is an infinite supply of the earth's goods." **(107).** Imposing this model on reality as a whole, human and social, leads to the deterioration of the environment. **(108).** The idea of promoting a different cultural paradigm partly independent of technology almost seems inconceivable today, since technology tends to absorb everything into its "ironclad logic." **(109).** Unfortunately, there is little interest in "more balanced levels of production, a better distribution of wealth, concern for the environment, and the rights of future generations." Maximizing profits is the dominant principle.

(110). It is imperative that data generated by other fields of knowledge (e.g., philosophy and social ethics) enter the development paradigm. **(111).** Seeking only a technical remedy to each environmental problem masks the deepest problems of the contemporary global system. **(112).** We must strive to broaden our vision so as to achieve true progress, which is "healthier, more human, more social, more integral." **(113).** Fortunately, there is "a growing awareness that scientific and technological progress cannot be equated with the progress of humanity and history." **(114).** There is an urgent need to move forward in a bold, cultural revolution; this involves controlling "our unrestrained delusions of grandeur."

III. The Crisis and Effects of Modern Anthropocentrism (115–121). **(115).** When human beings forget that they are God's gift, they fail to find their true place in the world; they need to respect their natural and moral structure with which they have been endowed. **(116).** Modernity has been marked by an excessive anthropocentrism. Human "dominion" over the universe is properly understood in the sense of "responsible stewardship." **(117).** If the inherent worth of the individual (e.g., a poor person, a human embryo, a disabled person) is not respected, the very foundations of our life begin to crumble. **(118).** There can be no renewal of our relationship with nature without a renewal of humanity itself. **(119).** Our relationship with the environment can never be isolated from our relationship with others and with God. **(120).** "Concern for the protection of nature is also incompatible with the justification of abortion." **(121).** The truths of Christianity seek a fruitful dialogue with changing historical situations.

Practical Relativism (122–123). (122). A misguided anthropocentrism leads to a misguided lifestyle. There is also a rise in relativism, which "sees everything as irrelevant unless it serves one's own immediate interests." This attitude leads to environmental degradation and social decay. **(123)**. The culture of relativism is the same disorder that drives one person to take advantage of another; this same thinking leads to a variety of social ills (e.g., the sexual exploitation of children, the abandonment of the elderly, the purchase of organs of the poor). Political efforts alone (without objective truths and sound principles) cannot prevent such abusive actions.

The Need to Protect Employment (124–129). (124). Any approach to an integral ecology asserts the value of labor. **(125).** All forms of labor connect us to others and to the world; this was clearly exemplified in the life of Charles de Foucauld. **(126).** The great monastic tradition combined prayer and spiritual reading with manual labor (*ora et labora*). **(127).** Work helps to integrate many aspects of life and society; thus, we prioritize the goal of steady employment for everyone. **(128).** We were created with the vocation to work; it gives meaning to life; it is a path to growth, human development, and personal fulfillment. **(129).** All honest forms of labor (e.g., agricultural, academic, business, etc.) serve the common good and seek to improve our world.

New Biological Technologies (130–136). (130). The human person is pivotal in a vision of creation. The Church's *Catechism* permits experimentation on animals within reasonable limits and if it contributes to saving human lives. **(131).** Any experimentation in one area of the ecosystem must pay due attention to its wider effects; indiscriminate genetic manipulation must be avoided. **(132).** Human intervention on plants and animals is legitimate if it is in line with the development of creation as intended by God. **(133).** Admittedly, it is difficult to make a general judgment about genetic modification. **(134).** Economic growth should promote the common good, not the concentration of land and possessions in the hands of a few. **(135).** Environmental issues are complex, requiring

constant attention and a concern for ethical implications. **(136).**
The inalienable worth of the human being sets boundaries, especially
for experimentation on living human embryos. Technology must
never be severed from ethics and moral principles.

CHAPTER FOUR: INTEGRAL ECOLOGY

(137). Pope Francis now focuses on an *integral ecology*, since
everything is closely interrelated and the world is facing a global crisis.

**I. Environmental, Economic, and Social Ecology
(138–142). (138).** Ecology studies show the interrelatedness
of all living organisms; this interconnectedness needs constant
emphasis. **(139).** The momentous challenges are *not* two separate
crises, one environmental and the other social; we face one complex
crisis. **(140).** How can we protect the world's ecosystems and
achieve a "sustainable" use of the earth's resources? **(141).** The
protection of the environment is an integral part of a holistic
development process; all fields of knowledge need to contribute to
finding solutions. These realities demonstrate the principle that "the
whole is greater than the part." **(142).** A genuine social ecology will
incorporate the whole of society from the primary social group of
the family to international communities.

II. Cultural Ecology (143–146). (143). Ecology also involves
protecting the cultural treasures of humanity in the broadest sense,
including past treasures and current realities. **(144).** Since life
and the world are dynamic realities, our care for the world must be
flexible and dynamic; this approach necessarily respects the rights
of peoples and their cultures. **(145).** Various intensive forms of
environmental exploitation both exhaust resources and undo social
structures that have shaped people's cultural identity. **(146).** Thus,
it is essential to show special care for indigenous communities and
their cultural traditions.

III. Ecology of Daily Life (147–155). (147). Authentic development seeks an integral improvement in the quality of human life, including our wise use of the environment. **(148).** With admirable creativity and generosity, many people have responded to various undesirable environmental challenges by fostering warm relationships and creating communities. **(149).** A fine example showing the power of love is found in some unstable neighborhoods of mega-cities where belonging and togetherness are fostered. **(150).** Constantly, we seek the unique beauty reflected in people's quality of life, their encounters and mutual assistance.

(151). In today's cities it is necessary to protect common areas, visual landmarks, and urban landscapes to create a sense of belonging, rootedness, and a "feeling at home." **(152).** The lack of adequate housing both in cities and rural areas affects one's sense of personal dignity and family life; this is a major issue for human ecology. **(153).** The quality of life in cities is greatly affected by systems of transport; public transport should be given priority. **(154).** The chaotic realities that people are forced to endure in city life negatively affect our dignity as human beings. **(155).** An "ecology of man" (Benedict XVI) means accepting our bodies as God's gift; everyone must value one's own body in its femininity and masculinity.

IV. The Principle of the Common Good (156–158). (156). Human ecology is inseparable from the notion of the common good, a central and unifying principle of social ethics. **(157).** Respect for the human person is the underlying principle of the common good. It is the duty of society, and the state in particular, to defend and promote the common good. **(158).** This basic principle is a summons to solidarity and a preferential option for the poorest of our brothers and sisters. A fundamental ethical imperative is essential for attaining the common good.

V. Justice between the Generations (159–162). **(159).** The notion of the common good also extends to future generations; sustainable development requires "intergenerational solidarity." Such solidarity is not optional; it is a basic question of justice. **(160).** Leaving an inhabitable planet to future generations is first and foremost our decision. **(161).** Unfortunately, "we may well be leaving to coming generations debris, desolation, and filth." The pace of consumption, waste, and environmental change has severely stretched the planet's capacity for viability. Decisive action is imperative. **(162).** The current ethical and cultural decline negatively impacts seriously addressing the environmental crisis; there is an urgent moral need to foster intergenerational solidarity!

CHAPTER FIVE: LINES OF APPROACH AND ACTION

(163). Having treated the present realities of environmental degradation, Pope Francis now outlines some major paths that can help us escape the spiral of self-destruction.

I. Dialogue on the Environment in the International Community (164–175). **(164).** There is a growing awareness that our planet is a homeland and that humanity is one people living in a common home; we are all interdependent. A global consensus is essential for confronting our deeper problems. **(165).** Sources of renewal energy are urgently needed to replace the use of highly polluting fossil fuels. Unfortunately, our age may well be remembered as "one of the most irresponsible in history." **(166).** Thanks to some farsighted approaches from various sectors, the ecological movement has made some significant advances. **(167).** Various World Summits have made progress in seeking to reverse the trends of global warming; however, these insights are often poorly implemented. **(168).** Important conventions have addressed subjects such as hazardous wastes, endangered species, and the ozone layer. **(169).** Other assemblies have discussed biodiversity, desertification, and climate change. However, significant progress is often delayed.

(170). Effective, implementable strategies for lowering pollutant gas emissions are urgently needed. Frequently, it is the poor who end up paying the greatest price. Countries who have benefitted most from industrialization have a greater responsibility for providing solutions. **(171).** The strategy of buying and selling "carbon credits" does little to solve root problems. **(172).** For poor countries, the priority must be the elimination of extreme poverty and the promotion of the social development of their people. The use of abundant solar energy needs development. **(173).** Enforceable international agreements are urgently needed. **(174).** The growing problem of marine waste and the protection of the open seas represent particular challenges. **(175).** Humanity needs "radical decisions to reverse the trend of global warming."

II. Dialogue for New National and Local Policies (176–181). (176). Resolving issues related to the environment and economic development needs effective policies on both national and local levels. **(177).** Guidelines for admissible environmental conduct must foster the common good; "best practices" need to be promoted. **(178).** It is important to realize that we "are always more effective when we generate processes, rather than holding on to positions of power." **(179).** Local individuals and groups can make a real difference. "Unless citizens control political power—national, regional, and municipal—it will not be possible to control damage to the environment." **(180).** Yet there are no uniform recipes because each locality has its own unique problems and limitations. **(181).** Continuity is essential, because policies related to environmental protection take time and long-term implementation.

III. Dialogue and Transparency in Decision-Making (182–188). (182). Environmental progress requires a free exchange of views; political corruption must be avoided. **(183)**. In seeking consensus on crucial questions, the local population should have a special place at the table, since they are most directly affected by decisions. **(184)**. Projects need in-depth study as to their effects on the quality of life. **(185)**. Any proposed venture must clearly answer a multitude of questions to ensure genuine integral development. **(186)**. The Rio Declaration of 1992 asserted that measures must always be in place to "prevent environmental degradation." **(187)**. We are not opposed to technological innovations, but "profit cannot be the sole criterion." **(188)**. Francis clearly states that "the Church does not presume to settle scientific questions or to replace politics."

IV. Politics and Economy in Dialogue for Human Fulfillment (189–198). (189). To promote the common good, politics and economics must enter into dialogue in the service of life, especially human life. **(190)**. Environmental protection cannot be determined solely by financial calculations; human impact questions must have primary importance. **(191)**. Asking fundamental questions does not mean blocking progress and human development; in fact, it may open pathways for a more genuine growth. **(192)**. Intelligently and responsibly promoting sustainable and equitable development is to be promoted within the broader concept of the quality of life. **(193)**. We must be open to setting reasonable limits on growth, encouraging more sober lifestyles, and reducing energy consumption and improving its efficiency.

(194). Our notion of progress needs evaluation. It must move beyond mere technological and economic development and promote a higher quality of human life; only then can it be considered genuine progress. **(195)**. The ethical dimensions of development must always enter the discussion and planning. **(196)**. The social principle of subsidiarity also needs to guide development plans. We also always ask how any plan affects the most vulnerable in society. **(197).** What is needed is a farsighted politics capable of new, integral, and interdisciplinary approaches to handling the different aspects of the crisis. **(198).** Politics and economics both must admit their own mistakes and find forms of interaction directed to the common good. The principle that "unity is greater than conflict" holds true in all discussion and planning.

V. Religions in Dialogue with Science (199–201). (199). It cannot be maintained that empirical science provides a complete explanation of life. For example, classical literature, both secular and religious, enables our ability to grasp the ultimate meaning and purpose of life. **(200).** Any technical solutions to environmental challenges will prove powerless "if humanity loses its compass." If people of faith constantly return to their sources, they will be better equipped to respond to today's urgent needs. **(201).** The majority of the world's people profess to be believers. All must enter into dialogue with several groups, including various sciences, ecological movements, and governments. The path of dialogue "requires patience, self-discipline, and generosity, always keeping in mind that 'realities are greater than ideas.'"

CHAPTER SIX: ECOLOGICAL EDUCATION AND SPIRITUALITY

(202). For an adequate protection of the environment, numerous changes are necessary; however, it is we human beings above all who need to change; a long path of renewal is demanded.

I. Toward a New Lifestyle (203–208). (203). The market constantly promotes extreme consumerism; compulsive consumerism is one example of how the techno-economic paradigm affects individuals. Humans need a new self-awareness. **(204).** When people become self-centered and self-enclosed, their greed increases; a genuine sense of the common good also disappears. **(205).** Yet all is not lost; we are capable of rising above ourselves and choosing what is good, never forgetting the dignity that is ours. **(206)**. A lifestyle change is imperative, always considering the environmental impact of production and consumption. **(207)**. The *Earth Charter* (2000) sought "the awakening of a new reverence for life." **(208)**. We are capable of going out of ourselves toward the other, rejecting every form of self-centeredness and self-absorption.

II. Educating for the Covenant between Humanity and the Environment (209–215). (209). An awareness of today's grave situation must be reflected in new habits; the mere amassing of things and pleasures does not bring joy to the heart. **(210)**. Environmental education needs a broad vision, including an openness to the transcendent; it must develop "an ethics of ecology." **(211)**. There is a nobility in caring for creation through daily, little actions (numerous concrete examples are provided). **(212)**. Such small efforts positively affect the wider world. **(213)**. Ecological education can take place in many diverse settings. For example, "In the face of the so-called culture of death, the family is the heart of the culture of life." **(214)**. A wide variety of institutions and social groups (including the Church) "have an important role to play in ecological education." **(215)**. Without a change of mindsets, the paradigm of consumerism will continue to advance.

III. Ecological Conversion (216–221). (216). The rich heritage of Christian spirituality has a precious contribution to make to the renewal of humanity, motivating us to a more passionate concern for the protection of our world. **(217)**. All need an ecological conversion springing from an encounter with Jesus Christ. **(218)**. Saint Francis of Assisi helps us to see that our personal conversion is linked to a healthy relationship with creation. **(219)**. In addition to personal renewal, social problems must be addressed by community networks. **(220)**. Numerous attitudinal changes are imperative. **(221)**. Various faith convictions, mentioned throughout the encyclical, help to nurture the sublime fraternity with all creation that Saint Francis of Assisi so radiantly embodied.

IV. Joy and Peace (222–227). **(222)**. Christian spirituality encourages a prophetic and contemplative lifestyle. We need to learn the ancient lesson that "less is more." **(223)**. A simple lifestyle is actually a way of living life to the full. **(224)**. Following faith convictions, we seek to both live and promote a kind of healthy humility and happy sobriety. **(225)**. Achieving inner peace is closely linked with care for ecology and the common good. **(226)**. A renewed "attitude of the heart" enables us to better contemplate nature's beauty. **(227)**. Simple practices such as prayer before and after meals recall our dependence on God and expresses gratitude for creation's gifts.

V. Civic and Political Love (228–232). **(228)**. Care for nature includes an awareness of God as our common Father, fostering a "universal fraternity." **(229)**. The conviction that we need one another and share responsibility for others and the world must increase. **(230)**. We seek to learn from Saint Thérèse of Lisieux, practicing the "little way of love." **(231)**. Authentic love affects not only relationships between individuals, but also "macro-relationships, social, economic, and political ones." Such love encourages a "culture of care" that permeates all of society. **(232)**. Countless organizations in diverse ways promote the common good and defend the environment. These community actions, when they express self-giving love, can also become intense spiritual experiences.

VI. Sacramental Signs and the Celebration of Rest (233–237). **(233)**. We are invited to discover God in all things— "in a leaf, in a mountain trail, in a dewdrop, in a poor person's face." **(234)**. This does not assert that finite things are divine, but that various mystic experiences enable us, as Saint John of the Cross taught, to appreciate that "all things are God." **(235).** The sacraments are a privileged way in which nature is taken up by God (e.g., water, oil, fire, etc.). Christians believe that all creatures of the material universe find their true meaning in the Incarnate Word. **(236).** It is in the Eucharist that all that has been created finds its greatest exaltation. The Eucharist joins heaven and earth; it embraces and penetrates all creation. **(237).** Sunday as a day of rest heals our relationships with God, with ourselves, with others, and with the world; it integrates the whole week and motivates us to a greater concern for nature and for the poor.

VII. The Trinity and the Relationship between Creatures (238–240). (238). In contemplating the wonder, grandeur, and beauty of the universe, we must praise the Trinity: Father, Son, and Spirit. **(239).** Saint Bonaventure taught that *each creature bears in itself a specifically Trinitarian structure*; thus, we are challenged to read reality in a Trinitarian key. **(240).** We are invited to develop "a spirituality of that global solidarity that flows from the mystery of the Trinity."

VIII. Queen of All Creation (241–242). (241). As Mary cared for Jesus, she now cares with maternal affection and pain for this wounded world. She is the Mother and Queen of all creation. **(242).** Saint Joseph cared for the Holy Family. The Gospel presents him as a just, hardworking man, who also "shows great tenderness, which is not a mark of the weak, but of those who are genuinely strong," ready to love and serve in humility.

IX. Beyond the Sun (243–245). (243). At the end of time, we will find ourselves face-to-face with the infinite beauty of God (cf. 1 Cor 13:12) and meet Jesus, who promises to "make all things new" (Rev 21:5). **(244).** As we journey through life, "let us sing as we go." May our struggles and concern for the planet never take away the joy of our hope. **(245).** In the heart of this world, the Lord of life accompanies us, for he has united himself definitely to our earth.

Two Final Prayers (246). At the end of this lengthy reflection, which has been both joyful and troubling, Pope Francis offers two prayers, one for all who believe in God, the other for Christians. *A Prayer for Our Earth.* All-powerful God, you are present in the whole universe.... Pour out upon us the power of your love.... Fill us with peace.... Bring healing to our lives.... Teach us to discover the worth of each thing.... Encourage us, we pray, in our struggle for justice, love, and peace. *A Christian Prayer in Union with Creation.* Father, we praise you with all your creatures.... Son of God, Jesus.... You were formed in the womb of Mary our Mother; you became part of this earth.... Praise be to you! Holy Spirit,... inspire us to do what is good.... Triune Lord,...teach us to contemplate you.... God of love, show us our place in this world as channels of your love.... O Lord,...help us to protect all life [as we await] the coming of your Kingdom of justice, peace, love, and beauty. Praise be to you! Amen.

5

Amoris Laetitia
The Joy of Love

(March 19, 2016)

Pope Francis has given the Church an extraordinary gift: *Amoris Laetitia—The Joy of Love*—a document focused on the family and love. It draws heavily on the 2014 and 2015 worldwide bishops' synods on the family; Pope Francis enriches the discussion with his deep pastoral insights. The English text runs to over 250 pages. Quotations are drawn from a wide variety of sources: earlier popes, Vatican II documents, various episcopal conferences, a variety of saints; it even cites Martin Luther King and the film *Babette's Feast*. Francis' letter sets an important pastoral agenda for the entire Church. He does not change any Church teaching but he expresses his pastoral wisdom by always emphasizing mercy and compassion, asserting that in all situations, "the Church is commissioned to proclaim the mercy of God, the beating heart of the Gospel" (309).

The Joy of Love begins with various biblical perspectives; "the Bible is full of families, births, love stories, and family crises" (8). In fact, "Jesus himself was born into a modest family" (21). "Every family should look to the icon of the Holy Family of Nazareth" (30). In great depth Francis explores the current situation of families, focusing on "concrete realities" in order to improve the Church's pastoral response, because he believes "the welfare of the family is decisive for the future of the world and that of the Church" (31). The pope recommends a rethinking of the Church's pastoral approaches to marriage and family life. For Francis, it is not enough to stress "doctrinal, bioethical, and moral issues"; the Church must encourage "openness to grace," asserting, "We have been called to form consciences, not to replace them" (37). Great sensitivity must be shown to those living in "irregular situations"; we must never use moral laws "as if they were stones to throw at people's lives" (305).

Pope Francis presents essential elements of the Church's teaching on marriage and the family, discussing such themes as indissolubility, the sacramental nature of marriage, the transmission of life, and the education of children. He does not change the Church's vision in regard to divorced Catholics, remarried Catholics, same-sex marriages, or homosexuality. Francis prefers always to emphasize that "our teaching on marriage and the family cannot fail to be inspired and transformed by the message of love and tenderness; otherwise, it becomes nothing more than the defense of a dry and lifeless doctrine" (59). Married life and the family are truly the "sanctuary of life" (83). Notice—and be enriched—by the pastoral, compassionate, and merciful tone of Pope Francis' teaching!

Amoris Laetitia
Synthesis Text

INTRODUCTION

The Joy of Love (1–7). (1). The joy of love experienced by families is also the joy of the Church; the Christian proclamation on the family is good news to all. **(2).** The 2014–2015 synod examined the situation of families in today's world, discussing doctrinal, moral, spiritual, and pastoral questions. **(3).** These many issues require solutions on local, country, or regional levels; Francis asserts that every issue need *not* be solved by the magisterium. **(4).** The two-year synod process proved both impressive and illuminating; it reflected on many legitimate concerns and honest questions. **(5).** This exhortation was promulgated during the Jubilee Year of Mercy (2015–2016); it encourages everyone to be signs of mercy wherever family life is imperfect or lacks peace and joy. **(6).** This document examines Scripture, actual family situations, the Church's teaching, and pastoral discernment. **(7).** The length of the document (nine chapters) reflects the fact that the synod evolved over two years; thus, it demands a leisurely reflective reading. All are called to realize that "families are not a problem; they are first and foremost an opportunity."

CHAPTER ONE: IN THE LIGHT OF THE WORD

(8). The Bible is full of families, births, love stories, and family crises. For example, Psalm 128:1–6 resounds in both Jewish and Christian wedding liturgies.

You and Your Wife (9–13). (9). Family life is designed to reflect God's plan, where a father and mother share their personal story of love (cf. Mt 19:4; Gen 2:24). **(10).** The early chapters of Genesis note that humans "male and female" were created in the "image of God" and were to be a sign of God's creative act. **(11).** The couple that loves and begets life is a true, living icon of God. "The triune God is a communion of love, and the family is its living reflection." **(12).** As noted in Genesis, man sought a "fitting helper," someone who would actually reflect God's own love. **(13).** Woman is given to man, relieving his solitude and giving rise to new birth and the family. They are to cleave to each other, voluntarily giving themselves in love, thus becoming one flesh.

Your Children Are as the Shoots of an Olive Tree (14–18). (14). In the home where husband and wife are seated at table, their children appear at their side "like olive shoots" (Ps 128:3);

children are like the "living stones" of the family (1 Pet 2:5). **(15).** The New Testament speaks of "churches that meet in homes" (e.g., 1 Cor 16:19; Rom 16:5; Col 4:15); thus, a family's living space can become a domestic church, a setting for the Eucharist where Christ is present. **(16).** The Bible also presents the family as the place where children are raised in the faith; parents are their children's first teachers in the faith. **(17).** Parents have the serious responsibility for the work of education, teaching them what to "honor one's father and mother" concretely means. **(18).** The Gospel reminds us that children are not the "property" of the family; their mission extends beyond the earthly family to hear the word of God and do it (cf. Lk 8:21).

A Path of Suffering and Blood (19–22). (19). Scripture also presents the truth that pain, evil, and violence can break up families and their communion of life and love. **(20).** This thread of suffering and bloodshed runs through numerous pages of the Bible (e.g., the patriarchs, King David, and Job). **(21).** Examples of suffering are seen in the Holy Family fleeing to Egypt, the pain of the widow of Nain, and the father of the epileptic child. **(22).** Thus, the Word of God can be a source of comfort for every family that experiences difficulties and suffering.

The Work of Your Hands (23–26). (23). From the very first pages of the Bible, work is portrayed as an essential part of human dignity (Ps 128:2). **(24).** Honest labor promotes the development of society and provides for the sustenance, stability, and fruitfulness of one's family. Saint Paul worked with his own hands, noting that "If anyone will not work, let him not eat" (2 Thess 3:10). **(25).** Great suffering results from unemployment and the lack of steady work, taking its toll on the serenity of family life. **(26).** Social degeneration caused by sin (e.g., abuse of the environment) causes additional family stress.

The Tenderness of an Embrace (27–30). (27). Christ proposed that the distinctive sign of his disciples would be their love and self-giving for others. Such love bears fruit in mercy and forgiveness. **(28).** Love also overflows in the virtue of tenderness. The prophet Hosea notes God's tender love for Israel, caressing and feeding the child Israel (Hos 11:1, 3–4). **(29).** Reflecting the love relationship of the Trinity, families mirror God's creative work in their begetting and raising of children. **(30).** Families should look to the icon of the Holy Family of Nazareth; they faced challenges with courage and serenity. Like Mary, they should treasure everything in their hearts.

CHAPTER TWO: THE EXPERIENCES AND CHALLENGES OF FAMILIES

(31). The welfare of the family is decisive for the future of the world and the Church. In this context, Pope Francis provides some pastoral insights that emerge from the synod discussion and his own personal experience.

The Current Reality of the Family (32–49). (32). The synod sought to reflect on the reality of today's family in all its complexity, including both its lights and shadows; among various emphases one finds the importance of better personal communication between the spouses. **(33).** Several cultural changes (e.g., heightened individualism) have brought new tensions to family life. **(34).** Another challenge comes from confused ideas about personal freedom and commitment. **(35).** Concerted effort by the Church is needed to present cogent reasons for choosing marriage and family life. **(36).** The Church needs "a healthy dose of self-criticism" to better enunciate a humble and realistic vision of marriage, avoiding "excessive idealization."

(37). In matters of marriage and family life, the Church needs "to make room for the consciences of the faithful." "We have been called to form consciences, not to replace them." **(38)**. Acknowledging positive factors, we are grateful for "the witness of marriages that have not only proved lasting, but also fruitful and loving." **(39)**. The synod noted the growing "cultural of the ephemeral," where everything becomes disposable and narcissism grows. **(40)**. Risking an oversimplification, it can be said that contemporary culture often pressures young people not to start a family. **(41)**. All face the growing spread of pornography and the commercialization of the body. Also, we note that resolving marital problems needs patience, sacrifice, and forgiveness.

(42). With decreasing population, the relationship between generations is no longer ensured. Consumerism may deter people from having children in order to maintain a certain freedom and lifestyle. The Church rejects forced State intervention in matters of contraception, sterilization, and even abortion. **(43)**. The weakening of faith and religious practice negatively affects the view of families, children, and the elderly. **(44)**. Lack of affordable housing has a negative impact, because "families and homes go together." **(45)**. The number of children born outside of wedlock is growing. There is the tragedy of the sexual abuse of children, particularly if it occurs "in families, schools, communities, and Christian institutions."

(46). Migration brings multiple serious challenges; organized human trafficking poses immense problems. Church programs to help families forgo migration are urgently needed. **(47)**. Persons with special needs and disabilities require added attention. Francis asserts that they are "a gift for the family and an opportunity to grow in love, mutual aid, and unity"; we desire that they be fully integrated into our communities. **(48)**. Many families lovingly care for their elderly and assure a dignified end of life. The Church views euthanasia and assisted suicide as serious threats and opposes them. **(49).** All need to show mercy and compassion to those living with great limitations (poverty, single parenthood); they must not be judged; they deserve our love.

Some Challenges (50–57). (50). Diverse situations pose challenges to family life (e.g., exhausted parents, no common meals, addiction to media and television). **(51).** Addictions to drugs, alcohol, and gambling often result in family breakdowns. Violence in the family results in distorted human relationships with long-term effects. **(52).** While recognizing the great variety of family situations, same-sex unions "may not simply be equated with marriage." No union closed to the transmission of life can ensure the future of society. **(53).** Some societies retain various traditional practices (polygamy, arranged marriages, etc.); these must be evaluated, leading to the discovery of the authentic meaning of marriage. The strength of the family "lies in its capacity to love and to teach how to love."

(54). There has been progress in the recognition of women's rights, yet much remains to be accomplished. We must see "in the women's movement the working of the Spirit for a clearer recognition of the dignity and rights of women." **(55).** Men play a pivotal role in family life. A father's absence, be it physical, emotional, psychological, or spiritual, "deprives children of a suitable father figure." **(56).** There are various forms of an ideology of gender with diverse consequences. It is necessary that we not fall into "the sin of trying to replace the Creator. We are creatures, and not omnipotent." **(57).** Francis says, "I thank God that many families… live in love, fulfill their calling, and keep moving forward, even if they fall many times along the way." Family ministry needs new forms of missionary creativity.

CHAPTER THREE: LOOKING TO JESUS: THE VOCATION OF THE FAMILY

(58). The beautiful message of the Gospel needs to resound widely; its message has to occupy the center of all evangelizing activity. (59). Church teaching on the family must manifest love and tenderness; otherwise, it becomes "dry and lifeless doctrine." Francis says that he wishes "to invoke the fire of the Spirit upon all the world's families." (60). This present, brief chapter summarizes "the Church's teaching on marriage and the family."

Jesus Restores and Fulfills God's Plan (61–66). (61). Marriage is to be seen as a gift from the Lord (1 Cor 7:7); thus, it is to be held in honor (Heb 13:4). (62). Jesus reaffirmed the indissoluble union of marriage (Mt 19:6) as part of God's original plan (cf. Mt 19:3). (63). Marriage and the family have been redeemed by Christ (cf. Eph 5:21–22); the spousal union takes on its full meaning in Christ and his Church. (64). Jesus' example is paradigmatic for the Church; he participated in the wedding at Cana; he had a deep friendship with the family of Lazarus and his sisters; he sympathized with grieving parents. (65). The Word became incarnate in a family, changing the history of the world. This mystery fascinated Francis of Assisi, Theresa of the Child Jesus, and Charles de Foucauld; it continues to fill Christian families with hope and joy. (66). Nazareth teaches us the meaning of family life, its communion, its beauty, and its sacred and inviolable character.

The Family in the Documents of the Church (67–70). (67). The Second Vatican Council sought to promote the dignity of marriage and the family (cf. GS 47–52); spouses build up the Body of Christ and form a domestic church (LG 11). (68). Pope Paul VI in *Humanae Vitae* brought out the intrinsic bond between conjugal love and the generation of life. (69). Pope John Paul II gave special attention to the family in his catechesis on human love; in *Familiaris Consortio* he defined the family as "the way of the Church." **(70).** Pope Benedict XVI stressed that marriage based on love becomes an icon of the relationship between God and his people.

The Sacrament of Matrimony (71–75). (71). The family is the image of God, who is a communion of persons. Jesus raised marriage to the sacramental sign of his love for the Church. **(72).** The sacrament of marriage is much more than a social convention; it is a vocation and a response to the call to experience conjugal love. **(73).** Mutual self-giving in marriage flows from the grace of Baptism. Christian marriage is a sign of how much Christ loved his Church. **(74).** Sexual union becomes a path of growth in the life of grace for the couple; both are responding to God's gift with commitment, creativity, perseverance, and daily effort. **(75).** In the Church's Latin tradition, the ministers of the Sacrament of Marriage are the man and woman who marry.

Seeds of the Word and Imperfect Situations (76–79). (76). Married couples seek to achieve a deeper grasp and a fuller integration of the mystery of marriage in their lives. **(77).** Forms of marriage in other cultures and religions need to be appreciated for the "seeds of the Word" they may contain. **(78).** The Church's pastoral care for the faithful who are living together, civilly married, divorced, or remarried must focus on compassion and encouragement for them to do good and lovingly care for each other. **(79).** When facing difficult situations, pastors must always exercise careful discernment and avoid making judgments; they need to appreciate how people experience and endure distress because of their life situation.

The Transmission of Life and the Rearing of Children (80–85). (80). Marriage is first an "intimate partnership of life and love"; thus, even childless couples can have a full conjugal life in both human and Christian terms. **(81).** The child is a gift, the fruit of the specific act of conjugal love of the parents, who are to be instruments of the Creator's love. **(82).** The Church's teaching is meant to help couples experience deep communion. As noted in *Humanae Vitae*, the dignity of the person must be respected in morally assessing methods of regulating birth. **(83).** Pope Francis asserts that "no alleged right to one's own body can justify a decision to terminate a life"; no person can be considered the "property" of another person. Human life must be protected at all stages of life, including its last. The Church "firmly rejects the death penalty." **(84).** The education of children is a most serious duty; it is the primary right of parents. **(85).** The Church seeks to join with parents in the fulfillment of their educational mission.

The Family and the Church (86–88). (86). The Church joyfully looks to families who remain faithful, becoming truly a "domestic church" (LG 11); here profound values are transmitted. **(87).** The Church as a family of families is constantly enriched by all these domestic churches. The Church is good for the family, and the family is good for the Church. **(88).** The experience of familial love is a perennial source of strength for the Church and society at large.

CHAPTER FOUR: LOVE IN MARRIAGE

(89). Necessarily, in speaking of marriage and the family, one must speak of love. The grace of the Sacrament of Marriage is to perfect the couple's love. As Saint Paul notes, "without love, I am nothing" (cf. 1 Cor 13:2–3). However, today the word "love" is often misused.

Our Daily Love (90). In the lyrical passage of Saint Paul (1 Cor 13:4–7), we find several features of true love. **Love Is Patient (91–92). (91).** This quality of love describes one who does not act on impulse and avoids giving offense; it reflects God's own patience and mercy toward sinners. **(92).** Unless we cultivate patience, we can always find excuses for responding negatively. Genuine love always includes deep compassion. **Love Is at the Service of Others (93–94).** **(93).** Patient love does not adopt a passive attitude; love is kind when it is ever ready to assist others. **(94).** Ignatius of Loyola noted that "love is shown more by deeds than by words." Genuine love derives pleasure from giving and serving.

Love Is Not Jealous (95–96). **(95).** A jealous or envious attitude is contrary to love; it closes us in on ourselves and leaves a sour taste; it produces a sadness provoked by another's prosperity. **(96).** Love inspires a sincere esteem for others, recognizing everyone's right to happiness. The Church is challenged to help society's outcasts find a modicum of joy. **Love Is Not Boastful (97–98).** **(97).** Love focuses on others, not oneself; it is not haughty, pedantic or pushy. One does not become inflated with one's self-importance. **(98).** Christians are to show concern for others, seeking to understand, forgive, and serve. Christian love is not about importance and power!

Love Is Not Rude (99–100). **(99).** True love is gentle and thoughtful, not rude, impolite, abrasive, or rigid. Love abhors making anyone suffer. Love waits until the other opens the door to his or her heart. **(100).** Being open to encountering others requires "a kind look." Jesus frequently spoke words of comfort, strength, consolation, and encouragement to others: "Go in peace" (Lk 7:50); "Be not afraid" (Mt 14:27). **Love Is Generous (101–102).** **(101).** Genuine love of self is a psychological prerequisite for being able to love others. **(102).** Thomas Aquinas noted that it is more proper to charity to desire to love than the desire to be loved. The greatest of loves can even lead to "laying down one's life" for another (cf. Jn 15:13).

Love Is Not Irritable or Resentful (103–104). **(103).** Interior irritation or hostility serves no one; if it permeates our attitude toward others, it is harmful. **(104).** We are challenged to never grow weary in doing good (Gal 6:9), to never be overcome by evil (Rom 12:21). Pope Francis gives this counsel: "My advice is never to let the day end without making peace in the family." We must "always say 'no' to violence in the home." **Love Forgives (105–108). (105).** Genuine forgiveness seeks to understand people's weaknesses and to excuse them. **(106).** Forgiveness is never easy; family communion is only preserved through the spirit of sacrifice. **(107).** Without forgiveness, we become distant from others and fearful in our interpersonal relationships. We need to learn to pray over our past history. **(108).** We deeply treasure our own experience of having been forgiven by God's unconditional love; we seek to show this love and forgiveness to others.

Love Rejoices with Others (109–110). (109). Valuing the dignity, abilities, and good works of others reflects genuine love. **(110).** Our Lord appreciates those who find joy in other's happiness; the family is to be a place that rejoices when something good happens to one of its members. **Love Bears All Things (111–113). (111).** Saint Paul's hymn notes that love *bears, believes, hopes,* and *endures* "all things." **(112).** Bearing all things implies control of one's tongue, limiting judgment, avoiding slander and gossip, and protecting the good name of others. **(113).** Loving, married couples avoid speaking of the spouse's limitations. "Love does not have to be perfect for us to value it." Though love may be imperfect this does not mean that it is untrue or unreal. "Love coexists with imperfection."

Love Believes All Things (114–115). (114). A believing love implicitly trusts others, seeing goodness even in darkness; it is "like an ember glowing beneath the ash." **(115).** Such love enables a relationship to be free; it does not try to control, possess, or dominate. This freedom fosters sincerity, transparency, and loving relationships in the family. **Love Hopes All Things (116–117). (116).** Love does not despair of the future, realizing that good can come out of difficult situations. **(117).** Christian hope embraces the certainty of life after death; all is transformed by Christ's resurrection. **Love Endures All Things (118–119). (118).** Love bears every trial with a positive attitude; this perspective is reflected in the words and vision of Martin Luther King, who sought to break the chain of hate. **(119).** Family life seeks to cultivate the strength of love, a love that never gives up.

Growing in Conjugal Love (120–122). (120). Our lengthy reflection on Saint Paul's hymn to love has prepared the path to discuss conjugal love; such love becomes an "affective union" that endures "long after emotions and passion subside." Conjugal love reaches its fullness in conjugal charity. **(121).** Marriage is a precious sign, an icon of God's love for us, mirrored in the unity of the Trinity. **(122).** Marriage entails a dynamic process, moving toward the progressive integration of God's gifts. **Lifelong Sharing (123–125). (123).** After the love that unites us to God, conjugal love is the greatest form of friendship. Those who witness the celebration of a loving union, however fragile, sincerely desire its permanence. **(124).** Love must grow strong to avoid succumbing to today's "culture of the ephemeral." Robert Bellarmine notes that faithful, marital love is actually a sign of a great mystery. **(125).** In addition, marriage is marked by a passion always directed to an ever more stable and intense union; marital love integrates the human and the divine.

Joy and Beauty (126–130). (126). In marriage, the joy of love needs to be cultivated; Thomas Aquinas noted that the word "joy" refers to an expansion of the heart. **(127).** Love and charity esteem the great worth of another person, contemplating and appreciating the other's innate beauty and sacredness. **(128).** The experience of love is expressed in one's "gaze" of others, even if they are infirm, elderly, or physically unattractive. Love opens one's eyes to see the great worth of another human being. **(129).** The most intense joys in life arise when we are able to elicit joy in others, as manifested by the generous cook in *Babette's Feast*. **(130).** In addition, joy also grows through pain and sorrow. **Marrying for Love (131–132). (131).** Marriage involves a mature, shared commitment to deeper growth in love and commitment to one another; it involves many obligations born of love itself. **(132).** Given the seriousness of the marriage commitment, it cannot be the fruit of a hasty decision, but neither can it be postponed indefinitely.

A Love That Reveals Itself and Increases (133–135). (133). Love must reveal itself in words and deeds. Family love must frequently use three words: Please, Thank you, and Sorry. Such expressions daily protect and nurture love. **(134).** Maturing in love involves a process of constant growth; a love that fails to grow is at risk. Daily acts of love become ever more frequent, intense, generous, tender, and cheerful. **(135).** Dreaming of an idyllic and perfect love is not helpful; one must be realistic about limits, defects, and imperfection—and then commit to growing together toward maturity.

Dialogue (136–141). (136). Dialogue is essential for experiencing, expressing, and fostering love in marriage and family life. **(137).** Quality time is needed for patient listening to another person's story, disappointments, fears, hopes, and dreams. **(138).** To give real importance to another person, we must acknowledge others' truth, putting ourselves in their shoes and trying to peer into their hearts. **(139).** Dialogue requires openness to changing and expanding one's ideas. One must learn to express one's thoughts and feelings without offending others. **(140).** Affection and concern for another facilitate a better understanding of what they are trying to communicate. **(141).** Through reading, personal reflection, prayer, and openness to the world, we develop our ability to communicate worthwhile and insightful content.

Passionate Love (142). The Second Vatican Council teaches that conjugal love embraces the whole person. Mystics have affirmed that supernatural love is expressed well using symbols found in marital love. **The World of Emotions (143–146). (143).** Desires, feelings, emotions, what ancients called "the passions," all have importance in married life. **(144).** As a human person, Jesus showed his emotions; his human heart was open to others, their joys and sorrows. **(145).** Experiencing an emotion is morally neutral; how one deals with it determines its moral value, as well as its impact on family life. **(146).** Authentic marital love seeks to benefit all of family life.

God Loves the Joy of His Children (147–149). (147). The Church is not opposed to human happiness; she only objects to destructive forms of pleasure and *eros*. **(148).** Education and training in the areas of emotions and instinct are necessary so that passions are channeled in beautiful and healthy ways, promoting family life in all its fullness. **(149).** We truly believe that God loves the enjoyment felt by human beings. **The Erotic Dimension of Love (150–152). (150).** God himself created sexuality; thus, sexual desire is not to be viewed negatively. **(151).** Sexuality is not a means of gratification or entertainment; it is an avenue of expressing love in which the human person becomes a gift. **(152).** The erotic dimension of love must be seen as a gift from God that enriches the relationship of the spouses.

Violence and Manipulation (153–157). (153). Following a positive vision of sexuality, we can approach the entire subject with a healthy realism, yet aware that it faces numerous challenges today. **(154).** Even within marriage, sex can become a source of suffering and manipulation, if it does not involve genuine communication between spouses. **(155).** Couples must avoid negativity (e.g., insatiability, domination) in their relationship, because it destroys the beauty of the conjugal union. **(156).** Every form of sexual submission must be clearly rejected; married love is founded upon a reciprocal donation of self. Saint Paul's advice in Ephesians 5:21–32 must be interpreted holistically. **(157).** Challenging factors in the sexual relationship must not lead to negative views of sexuality in general. We must never forget that our human equilibrium is fragile and requires constant growth.

Marriage and Virginity (158–162). (158). Many unmarried people render great service to their own family, the Church, and the wider community. **(159).** Virginity is an authentic form of love; it speaks of the Kingdom and devotion to the Gospel. There is no inferiority or superiority regarding marriage or virginity and celibacy; these different states of life complement each other. **(160).** Spiritual perfection is focused on one's total life based on the evangelical councils. **(161).** Both virginity and conjugal love reflect Gospel values; both are simply different ways of loving. **(162).** Celibacy must avoid becoming "a comfortable single life." Celibates can be inspired by the selfless and loving service rendered by married persons. Secularization has often obscured the value of lifelong commitments.

The Transformation of Love (163–164). (163). Longer life spans now mean that close and exclusive relationships must last— even up to six decades. Feelings may change as life unfolds; thus, the love couples pledge is greater than any emotion, feeling, or state of mind, although it may include all of these. **(164).** Authentic love of another person includes different dimensions and new situations; it needs prayer to the Holy Spirit to survive and thrive.

Chapter Five: Love Made Fruitful

(165). Love always gives life. Children are living reflections of the love of a father and a mother, a permanent sign of their conjugal unity. **Welcoming a New Life (166–167). (166).** The family is the setting in which a new life is not only born, but is also welcomed as a gift of God. Even in difficult circumstances, the child is to be welcomed with openness and affection so it may reach its ultimate fulfillment. **(167).** While large families are a joy for the Church, this does not imply "unlimited procreation."

Love and Pregnancy (168–171). (168). Pregnancy is both a difficult and wonderful time, during which a woman shares in the mystery of creation. We believe that each child has a place in God's heart from all eternity. **(169).** A pregnant woman can participate in God's plan by dreaming of her child; true families are built on dreams. **(170).** Scientific advances can reveal much of the child's identity before birth, yet only the Father, the Creator, fully knows the child. Truly, each child is a gift, unique and irreplaceable! **(171).** Francis writes, "With great affection I urge all future mothers: keep happy and let nothing rob you of the interior joy of motherhood," asking the Lord to preserve your joy, so you can pass it on to your child.

The Love of a Mother and a Father (172–177). (172). Parental love is shown to the child in countless ways: their personal name, looks of love, smiles, embraces, and so on. Each child needs the love of both father and mother; such love manifests the very face of God. **(173).** The sense of being "orphaned" deeply affects the child; the weakening of the maternal presence "poses a grave risk to our world." **(174).** Mothers are the strongest antidote to the spread of self-centered individualism. Francis says, "Dear mothers: thank you," for your contribution to the Church and the world. **(175).** Mothers help children develop a capacity for intimacy and empathy; fathers enable children to face the challenges of the wider world. In addition, there is also welcomed flexibility of parental roles and responsibilities. **(176).** Unfortunately, Western culture often reflects "a society without fathers"—with deleterious effects. **(177).** God sets the father in the family to give his personal masculine gifts and foster the healthy growth of all children.

An Expanding Fruitfulness (178–184). (178). Marriage retains its character of being a communion of life and love—even when some couples remain childless. **(179).** Adoption is a very generous way to be parents; it is a praiseworthy option that manifests generosity—especially to unwanted or abandoned children. **(180).** The choice of adoption and foster care expresses a unique kind of marriage fruitfulness; it focuses on the best interests of the child. Concomitantly, the trafficking of children must be vigorously combatted. **(181).** Christian families should never forget that parenting involves fulfilling social obligations. **(182).** Jesus' own family was close to other families, relatives and friends, as well as a normal part of the community. **(183).** Families are also called to reach out to the needy, outcasts, and the poor through friendship and service; this generosity contributes to a happy family. **(184).** By their witness and words, families speak of Jesus to others, seeking to make God's love present in society.

Discerning the Body (185–186). (185). Saint Paul addresses a shameful situation in the Corinthian community (1 Cor 11:17–34), where the wealthier members discriminate against the poorer ones. **(186).** The Eucharist demands that we "discern" and form one body of the Church without distinctions and divisions, thus leading to a worthy reception of the sacrament.

Life in the Wider Family (187). The nuclear family needs to interact with the "wider family": relatives, cousins, and even neighbors, taking care of any of their special needs. **Being Sons and Daughters (188–190). (188).** We can never abandon our parents who gave us life; we are all sons and daughters. **(189).** The Fourth Commandment requires honoring one's father and mother; the virtuous bond between generations guarantees a truly humane society. **(190).** Children leave their parents to marry and establish a new home, but they never abandon them. Marriage challenges husbands and wives to find new ways of being sons and daughters.

The Elderly (191–193). (191). God asks us to hear both the cry of the poor and the cry of the elderly, making them feel a living part of the community. Francis states that he would like a Church that "challenges the throwaway culture" so that both young and old joyfully embrace each other. **(192).** The elderly foster the continuity of generations, often handing down important values to their grandchildren, including the faith. **(193).** Memory is necessary for growth. Listening to the "living memory" of the elderly assures the future of the family.

Being Brothers and Sisters (194–195). (194). The bond of fraternity between siblings is a great school of freedom and peace. The family introduces fraternity into the world. **(195).** Growing up with brothers and sisters fosters a beautiful experience of caring and helping one another; the experience is a true school of socialization. **A Big Heart (196–198). (196).** The larger human family (friends and other families) brings needed support in a variety of circumstances. **(197).** This larger family provides love and support to many (e.g., single mothers, parentless children, persons with disabilities, the unmarried, the separated or widowed, etc.). **(198).** The larger family includes all the in-laws. Love means *not* viewing them as somehow competitors, threats, or intruders; their traditions and customs are respected.

Chapter Six: Some Pastoral Perspectives

(199). The synod on the family raised the need for new pastoral methods. Francis notes these briefly, but focuses his reflections on some more significant pastoral challenges.

Proclaiming the Gospel of the Family Today (200–204). (200). Christian families are agents of the apostolate primarily through "their joy-filled witness as domestic churches." Pastoral planning needs better efforts at evangelization and catechesis inside the family. **(201).** The Gospel of the family responds to deep human expectations; it proposes values needed today, even in highly secularized societies. **(202).** The pastoral care of families is primarily parish-centered. Ordained ministers often lack adequate training to address family issues. **(203).** Seminarians need inter-disciplinary, not merely doctrinal, formation; they should balance time in the seminary with time in parishes. Laypersons, families, and women should be present in formation programs. **(204).** Lay leaders can assist in the pastoral care of families, especially in cases of domestic violence and sexual abuse.

Preparing Engaged Couples for Marriage (205–211). **(205).** The Church needs to help young people discover the dignity and beauty of marriage. **(206).** Programs of marriage preparation may follow various patterns. **(207).** The focus should be on helping couples make a solid beginning of their family life. **(208).** The primary objective of the preparation is to help each person learn how to love one's lifelong partner. Those best prepared for marriage have learned its values from their own parents. **(209).** Marriage preparation also helps couples recognize eventual problems and risks; they should discuss their expectations and the meaning of love and commitment. **(210).** Couples need to be able to detect danger signals in their relationship and possible solutions. **(211).** A "pedagogy of love" is needed in marriage preparation, including practical programs, sound advice, and psychological guidance.

The Preparation of the Celebration (212–216). (212). Numerous details are involved in preparing the wedding celebration. Couples are encouraged to avoid being swallowed up by "a society of consumption and empty appearances," opting for a more modest celebration. **(213).** The couple is encouraged to personally experience the meaning of each of the signs of the marriage liturgy. **(214).** The words of consent include all future realities.

Fidelity to one's promises "cannot be bought and sold"; they can only be maintained with sacrifice. **(215)**. The marriage sacrament is not only a single moment; it is a reality that permanently influences the whole of married life. **(216)**. The couple needs to meditate on the biblical readings, to learn to pray together, to consecrate their love before an image of the Virgin Mary, recalling Jesus' presence at the wedding of Cana.

Accompanying the First Years of Married Life (217–222). **(217)**. Marriage is a matter of love; only those who freely choose and love one another can marry. This conscious decision needs to be deepened—especially in the first years of marriage. **(218)**. Marriage is not something that happens once for all; it is a lifelong project. **(219)**. The couple's experience of love must not grow stagnant. "Young love needs to keep dancing toward the future with immense hope." **(220)**. Growth in married love demands generosity and sacrifice, constant "negotiation" so that both partners are always "winners." **(221)**. Partners need to have realistic expectations, understanding that married life is a process of growth; thus, love demands a kind of craftsmanship. **(222)**. Aspects of family planning require consensual dialogue between partners. There is much wisdom in Church documents (e.g., *Humanae Vitae* and *Familiaris Consortio*). Children are a wonderful gift from God and a joy for parents and the Church.

Some Resources (223–230). **(223)**. The initial years of marriage are a sensitive period, requiring pastoral accompaniment and supported by family spirituality, prayer, devotional practices, and Sunday Eucharist. **(224)**. Growth in love needs space and quality time together. **(225)**. Practical suggestions fostering family solidarity and communication include: free time together, recreation with the children, and celebration of family events. **(226)**. Other solidarity-building initiatives may include: sharing household chores, a morning kiss or evening blessing, and an occasional party. **(227)**. Fostering the growth in faith in the family can be accomplished through frequent confession, spiritual direction, and occasional retreats, because "the family that prays together stays together." **(228)**. Even if one spouse is not interested in the faith, common values can be found, remembering that love is always a gift of God. **(229)**. Various parish initiatives can be supportive of families, including marriage counseling and social services addressing a variety of family problems. **(230)**. Overall, "nowadays, pastoral care for families has to be fundamentally missionary, going out to where people are."

Casting Light on Crisis, Worries, and Difficulties. (231). Just as good wine matures, so the daily experience of fidelity gives married life richness and "body." **The Challenge of Crises (232–238)**. **(232)**. Surmounting a crisis in marriage can actually improve the couple's union. **(233)**. If problems are not dealt with, communication begins to suffer and distance grows. **(234)**. Crises need to be faced together. Authentic communication is an art to be learned—and practiced in moments of difficulty. **(235)**. The various stages of married life present new and unique challenges. **(236)**. Diverse personal crises (e.g., emotional, social, and spiritual) affect the life of the couple; these demand dialogue and the ability to forgive. **(237)**. Tensions in marriage, rather than threatening love, can serve as occasions for reviving and renewing it. **(238)**. After every crisis, couples can renew their "yes" and reaffirm their love. The Church urgently needs a ministry to assist those whose marital relationship has broken down.

Old Wounds (239–240). **(239)**. Marital problems may emerge due to the lack of maturity and negative emotions. **(240)**. Many people leave childhood without ever having felt unconditional love; they have also had poor relationships with family members. These difficulties, if left unhealed, can reemerge and hurt a marriage. **Accompaniment after Breakdown and Divorce (241–246). (241).** In cases of marital breakdown, separation may be inevitable and sometimes even necessary. **(242).** Pastoral care of the separated, divorced, or abandoned is needed, especially for the poor and vulnerable. **(243).** Those who have divorced and remarried should be made to feel part of the Church; "they are not excommunicated." **(244).** Church procedures to procure nullity need to be more accessible and less time-consuming. **(245).** In cases of separation or divorce, the welfare of the children must be the primary concern. **(246).** Supporting wounded parents is also very beneficial for the children. The Church is to diligently work to combat the increasing number of divorces.

Certain Complex Situations (247–252). (247). Issues involving diverse forms of mixed marriages require attention; the uniqueness of each situation needs careful consideration. **(248).** Marriages involving disparity of cult offer an opportunity for interreligious dialogue in everyday life. **(249).** Pastoral discernment is always needed in numerous complicated situations. **(250).** The Church seeks to imitate Jesus' boundless love for all persons without exception "regardless of sexual orientation," always respecting his or her human dignity. **(251).** Unions between homosexual persons are not to be placed on the same level as marriage. **(252).** Single-parent families result from a variety of causes; these parents must receive encouragement and support from other families in the Christian community.

When Death Makes Us Feel Its Sting (253–258). (253). When a loved one passes, the Church needs to meet this pastoral opportunity. **(254).** Jesus was deeply moved by the death of a friend; he wept (Jn 11:1–44). Losing a spouse or a child is particularly difficult. **(255).** Understandably, the grieving process takes a fair amount of time. With sincere compassion and the patient process of prayer, acceptance is achieved and peace returns. **(256).**

We are consoled, knowing that those who die do not completely pass away. Christians are strengthened by the promise of future immortality, believing that life is changed, but not ended. **(257).** We can maintain our solidarity with our loved ones by praying for them. Saint Thérèse of Lisieux said she wished to continue doing good from heaven. **(258).** By accepting the reality of death, we can prepare for it, readying ourselves to meet our deceased loved ones in heaven.

CHAPTER SEVEN: TOWARDS A BETTER EDUCATION OF CHILDREN

(259). Parents have an important influence on the moral development of their children—for better or for worse. Francis seeks to discuss how parents carry out their role consciously, enthusiastically, reasonably, and appropriately.

Where Are Our Children? (260–262). (260). Parents need to devote time to their children to shield them from harm, making the family a place of support, guidance, and direction. **(261).** The role of parents is not to control every situation, but to assist the children to grow in freedom, maturity, overall discipline, and real autonomy. **(262).** Children need loving guidance to grow in the responsible use of freedom so as to face life issues with good sense and intelligence.

The Ethical Formation of Children (263–267). (263). Parents can never completely delegate the moral formation of their children to others. **(264).** In addition, parents are responsible for shaping the will of their children, fostering good habits and a natural inclination to goodness. **(265).** A good ethical education includes helping a person to appreciate that it is in one's own interest to do what is right. **(266).** Good habits need to be developed, such as readily saying "Please," "Thank you," and "Sorry." **(267).** Moral education seeks to develop responsible freedom and virtue, described as "a conviction that has become a steadfast inner principle of operation."

The Value of Correction as an Incentive (268–270). **(268).** It is pivotal to help children realize that misbehavior has consequences, training them to ask forgiveness and to repair any harm done to others. **(269).** Parents need to show appreciation to their children so they will sense their parents' constant, patient trust. They must also teach their children not to get carried away by anger. **(270).** Discipline should not lead to discouragement, but instead be a stimulus to further progress and growth.

Patient Realism (271–273). (271). Moral education gradually progresses through small steps that can be understood, accepted, and appreciated by the young; this includes making proportionate sacrifices. **(272).** Ethical education has the positive value of helping the young grow in the ability to understand and live in peace with others and the larger community. **(273).** In proposing moral values, a slow and steady process is needed, taking into consideration the child's age and abilities; it also appreciates the contributions of psychology and the educational sciences.

Family Life as an Educational Setting (274–279). (274). The family is the first school of human values, where the proper use of freedom and media messages can be learned. **(275).** An important task of families is to educate in hope, teaching children how to defer desires, to practice self-mastery, and to be detached from one's impulses. **(276).** The family is the primary setting for learning socialization and avoiding self-absorption. **(277).** Families are pivotal in forming habits of consumption and of fostering care for the environment as our common home. **(278).** The maturing process can be helped or hindered by contemporary communication and entertainment media. **(279).** Domineering parents hamper the growth to affective maturity. Parents can receive great assistance from Christian communities as well as Catholic schools.

The Need for Sex Education (280–286). **(280).** Vatican II spoke of the need for "a positive and prudent sex education." This task is crucially important in an age where sexuality often tends to be trivialized and impoverished. **(281).** Sex education needs to come at a proper time and in a manner suited to the age of young people. **(282).** Fostering a healthy sense of modesty has immense value. **(283).** A distorted view overly emphasizes "safe sex." Sensitivity to various expressions of love and meaningful communication are to be communicated. **(284).** Formation initiatives need to help young people distinguish physical, sexual attraction from mature, authentic love. **(285).** Sex education includes appreciation of differences (e.g., the human body as male or female). **(286).** One's identity is the result of more than biological factors; it includes, among many factors, family history, culture, experience, personal friends, and formative situations.

Passing on the Faith (287–290). **(287).** Raising children calls for an orderly process of handing on the faith; such family catechesis presumes that parents themselves genuinely trust God. **(288).** Parents desirous of nurturing their children's faith are sensitive to their unique patterns of growth. **(289).** This commitment actually helps the whole family in its evangelizing mission. **(290).** The Church's pastoral care of families facilitates the communication of the faith, including social transformation and the care of creation. This commitment enables families to become both domestic churches and a leaven of evangelization in society.

CHAPTER EIGHT: ACCOMPANYING, DISCERNING AND INTEGRATING WEAKNESS

(291–292). **(291).** The Church approaches with love those who participate in her life in an incomplete manner, acting like a "field hospital." This theme was emphasized during the Jubilee Year devoted to mercy (2015–2016). **(292).** Christian marriage as a permanent union reflects the union between Christ and his Church, though some forms of contemporary union radically contradict this ideal.

Gradualness in Pastoral Care (293–295). (293). The Synod Fathers noted that people in imperfect marriage situations "need pastoral care that is merciful and helpful." **(294).** Numerous cultural factors and social circumstances influence people's choice to enter into various unions; "these couples need to be welcomed and guided patiently and discreetly." **(295).** As Pope John Paul II proposed in the so-called law of gradualness, the human being "knows, loves, and accomplishes moral good by different stages of growth."

The Discernment of "Irregular" Situations (296–300). (296). The synod addressed various situations of human imperfection, always emphasizing that the Church seeks to follow Jesus' way of mercy. **(297).** Everyone deserves the compassion of the Christian community as they struggle to reach the fullness of God's plan for them. **(298).** The divorced who have entered a new union "should not be pigeonholed"; they need compassionate assistance, especially when there are children from this second union. **(299).** Francis notes his agreement with many Synod Fathers who observed that ways and means are needed to integrate the remarried more fully into the Christian community. **(300).** This exhortation is not meant to supply new rules; personal discernment and pastoral discernment are constantly needed. No one should think that "the Church maintains a double standard" in its pastoral approaches.

Mitigating Factors in Pastoral Discernment (301–303). (301). Special discernment of difficult situations remains essential. "Hence, it can no longer simply be said that all those in any 'irregular' situation are living in a state of mortal sin." **(302).** The

Church's *Catechism* refers to circumstances that mitigate moral responsibility; individuals need to follow their conscience. **(303).** All discernment is dynamic and ongoing; an individual needs to ask what God himself is asking amid the concrete complexity of one's limits.

Rules and Discernment (304–306). (304). Recall the teaching of Saint Thomas Aquinas, who asserted that general principles are necessary, but "in matters of action, truth or practice, rectitude is not the same for all." **(305).** Francis notes that "a pastor cannot feel that it is simply enough to apply moral laws to those living in 'irregular' situations, as if they were stones to throw at people's lives." Discernment always seeks ways of helping people respond to God's call. **(306).** Fraternal charity, the *via caritatis*, is the first law of Christians (cf. Jn 15:12; Gal 5:14).

The Logic of Pastoral Mercy (307–312). (307). Seeking to avoid any confusion, Francis points out that the Church does not desist in proposing the full ideal of marriage. In addition, concerted pastoral effort is needed to strengthen marriages and prevent their breakdown. **(308).** Certainly, Jesus wants a Church attentive to people's goodness, "even if in the process, her shoes get soiled by the mud of the street." The Church needs "to enter into the reality of other people's lives and to know the power of tenderness. Whenever we do so, our lives become wonderfully complicated." **(309).** "The Church is commissioned to proclaim the mercy of God, the beating heart of the Gospel." **(310).** "We are called to show mercy because mercy was first shown to us…, for mercy is the very foundation of the Church's life." **(311).** The Church must always "make room for God's unconditional love in our pastoral activity." **(312).** We are asked to "open our hearts to those living on the outermost fringes of society" and integrate them into the Church.

CHAPTER NINE: THE SPIRITUALITY OF MARRIAGE AND THE FAMILY

(313). Charity takes on different hues, depending on one's calling and state of life. The Second Vatican Council presented the spirituality born of family life. We can describe certain basic characteristics of this spirituality that unfolds in family life and its relationships.

A Spirituality of Supernatural Communion (314–316). (314). Arising from the Trinity, God dwells deep within the marital love that gives him glory. (315). Marital spirituality reveals the Lord's presence in concrete families through thousands of small but real loving gestures. (316). A positive experience of family communion opens us to God and to others. Benedict XVI pointed out that "closing our eyes to our neighbor also blinds us to God."

Gathered in Prayer in the Light of Easter (317–318). (317). If a family is centered on Christ, he will unify and illumine its entire life, manifested in "moments of joy, relaxation, celebration, and even sexuality." (318). Family prayer expresses its Paschal faith through devotion to Our Lady, shared Eucharist, and "various expressions of popular piety [that] are a treasure of spirituality for many families."

A Spirituality of Exclusive and Free Love (319–320). (319). Marriage expresses the experience of completely belonging to another person, mutual support, and aging together; each spouse becomes "a sign and instrument of the closeness of the Lord, who never abandons us." (320). A healthy autonomy grows through love, when each spouse realizes that the other is not his or her own personal possession. This is "spiritual realism"; it demands "interior divestment"—and the assistance of the Holy Spirit.

A Spirituality of Care, Consolation, and Incentive (321–324). (321). Christian couples are cooperators of grace and witnesses of the faith for each other, their children, and relatives.

They reflect divine love in ordinary ways—a word, a look, a helping hand, a caress, an embrace. **(322).** All family life is a "shepherding" in mercy; through one's love and care, one leaves a mark on the life of others. **(323).** It is a profound spiritual experience to contemplate our loved ones with the eyes of God and to see Christ in them. This gives rise to a tenderness that can "stir in the other the joy of being loved." **(324).** A loving family goes forth, caring for others, seeking their happiness, and manifesting hospitality, especially to the poor and the neglected. Such a family becomes "a symbol, witness, and participant in the Church's motherhood."

Concluding Meditation (325). All need to rediscover the richness of the teachings of Jesus (cf. Mt 22:30) and Saint Paul (cf. 1 Cor 7:29–31). This exhortation has often noted that no family drops from heaven perfectly formed; families need constantly to grow and mature in their ability to love. "Let us make this journey as families, let us keep walking together.... May we never lose heart!"

Prayer to the Holy Family. "Jesus, Mary, and Joseph… to you we turn with trust. Holy Family of Nazareth, grant that our families too may be… authentic schools of the Gospel and small domestic churches. Holy Family of Nazareth, may families never again experience violence, rejection and division.... Holy Family of Nazareth, make us once more mindful of the sacredness and inviolability of the family, and its beauty in God's plan. Jesus, Mary, and Joseph, graciously hear our prayer. Amen."

6

Gaudete et Exsultate
Rejoice and Be Glad

(May 19, 2018)

Gaudete et Exsultate (GE) is the third Apostolic Exhortation issued by Pope Francis, following *Evangelii Gaudium* (2013) and *Amoris Laetitia* (2016). It is a call to holiness of life, clearly echoing the invitation found in Vatican II's *Lumen Gentium* Chapter 5 (numbers 39–42) with the title "The Universal Call to Holiness in the Church." Francis, often called a "man of Vatican II," continues his concerted efforts to fully implement the renewed vision of the Church emerging from the Council. GE is a medium-length document presented in five chapters; it is dated March 19, the feast of Saint Joseph, the anniversary of his inauguration as pope in 2013. Its title emerges from Scripture, specifically Matthew 5:12, where Jesus advises his disciples to "rejoice and be glad"—even in the midst of life's trials.

Key themes emerge in this inviting document. There are many forms of holiness; thus, each person is to discover one's particular pathway. Francis emphasizes the holiness in our "next-door neighbors," including parents, workers, the sick, and the elderly. There are modern enemies of holiness, particularly Gnosticism and Pelagianism. Of course, holiness follows Jesus' example in his life and teaching, particularly the Beatitudes (Mt 5:3–12). Spiritual attitudes highlighted by Francis include perseverance, patience, meekness, joy, and a sense of humor, boldness, and passion. Undoubtedly, there will be numerous challenges to living the Christian life; we need to turn to Mary, who authentically lived the Beatitudes of Jesus.

In GE Francis is seeking to make the "call to holiness" very practical and livable in daily life. He admits that this document is not a total synthesis of holiness or spirituality. While we can look to the saints for inspiration and examples, each is to develop one's unique way of living the Christian life. Prayer, Scripture, Eucharist, community, mission, Mary, and the saints all enter into the spiritual journey. In this spiritual commitment, everyone needs to be cognizant of the difficulties to be faced; however, Francis admits that "God asks everything of us, yet he also gives everything to us" (175).

Gaudete et Exsultate Synthesis Text

INTRODUCTION

(1). The Lord asks much from us; he calls us to holiness. **(2).** This document is not a complete overview of holiness or spirituality; its focus is on the practical living out of our Christian calling.

CHAPTER ONE: THE CALL TO HOLINESS

The Saints Who Encourage and Accompany Us (3–5). (3). Old Testament figures are part of the "great cloud of witnesses" (including our own mothers and grandmothers) that inspire us and urge us to keep moving forward. **(4).** We are in the company of the great saints, martyrs, and witnesses who sustain us in our journey. **(5).** The exemplary imitation of Christ by the saints has been recognized by the Church through beatification and canonization.

The Saints "Next Door" (6–9). (6). The Holy Spirit bestows abundant holiness on members of God's people; God desires an authentically holy people. **(7).** Holiness is manifested in many forms, often in our "next-door neighbors" who live "the middle class of holiness." **(8).** We look to examples of holiness in ordinary people; one example is Saint Teresa Benedicta of the Cross (Edith Stein). **(9).** Holiness is "the most attractive face of the Church," speaking powerfully to a wide variety of people.

The Lord Calls (10–13). (10). Vatican II forcefully stated that all the faithful, each in one's particular way, are called by the Lord. **(11).** Each person is to discern one's own path, bringing out the best and using God's generous gifts. **(12).** The "genius of women" (several individuals are cited) has contributed to vigor and renewal in the Church. **(13).** We are encouraged to give our all and embrace God's unique plan for us.

For You Too (14–18). (14). Whether one is married, religious, a laborer, parent, or grandparent, each is called to holiness. **(15).** Undoubtedly, the Church is both holy and sinful, yet she possesses helpful gifts, such as Scripture, the sacraments, and living communities. **(16).** Holiness, the call of the Lord, grows through repeated small gestures in daily life. **(17).** Life presents various difficulties; the challenge is to find a more perfect way of doing what one is already doing. **(18).** We are capable of loving with the Lord's unconditional love; this demonstrates God's power at work in us—even in the midst of human weakness.

Your Mission in Christ (19–24). (19). Clearly, one's mission on earth is to walk the path of holiness. **(20).** We unite ourselves with the Lord's death and resurrection, seeking to incarnate them in our choices and attitudes (as Saint Ignatius of Loyola pointed out). **(21).** True holiness is nothing other than charity lived to the full. **(22).** The Lord speaks to us through his saints and the totality of their lives. **(23).** Daily, we ask the Spirit to show us what Christ expects of us. **(24).** We are to be transformed and renewed by the Spirit and thus fulfill our mission.

Activity That Sanctifies (25–31). (25). One's mission is intimately connected to building Christ's kingdom of love, justice, and universal peace. **(26).** It is unhealthy to seek silence and avoid others, to seek prayer while distaining service. **(27).** We always remember that life does not merely have a mission, but always is a mission. **(28).** It is valid to speak of a spirituality of mission (*Evangelii Gaudium*), an ecological spirituality (*Laudato Si*), a spirituality of family life (*Amoris Laetitia*). **(29).** Finding moments of quiet, solitude, and silence before God is often difficult, but it proves most fruitful. **(30).** Distractions are omnipresent in today's world and affect our sense of mission and commitment to service of others. **(31).** We need a spirit of holiness to strengthen our solitude and service, our personal life and evangelizing efforts.

More Alive, More Human (32–34). (32). Let us not fear holiness; it will not take away any of one's energy, vitality, or joy. This is shown in the African "slave-saint" Josephine Bakhita. **(33).** Growth in holiness bears great fruit; an evangelized disciple becomes an empowered evangelizer. **(34).** We seek to set our sights high, recalling the words of León Bloy: "the only great tragedy in life is not to become a saint."

Chapter Two: Two Subtle Enemies of Holiness

(35). Two forms of false holiness can lead one astray: Gnosticism and Pelagianism. They are heresies, deceptive ideas, leading one away from Christ and others. **Contemporary Gnosticism. (36).** Gnosticism focuses on a personal, subjective faith; it imprisons one in his or her own thoughts and feelings.

An Intellect without God and without Flesh (37–39). (37). A person's perfection is not measured by the information or knowledge one possesses (Gnosticism); such a religion becomes incapable of touching Christ's suffering flesh in others. **(38).** Unfortunately, Gnosticism poses a deceptive attraction for some people. **(39).** The Church employs a healthy and humble use of reason to deepen its understanding of the faith and the Gospel.

A Doctrine without Mystery (40–42). (40). Gnosticism is dangerous since it considers its own vision of reality to be perfect and fosters a disembodied spirituality. **(41).** Undoubtedly, God infinitely transcends us and is full of surprises; we cannot determine how and when we will encounter him; we do not control God. **(42).** A Gnostic mentality does not accept that God is mysteriously present in the life of every person.

The Limits of Reason (43–46). (43). Pope Francis notes that in the Church there are legitimate diverse interpretations of many aspects of doctrine and Christian life. **(44).** There is legitimate diversity in the Church and in the understanding and expression of its teachings. **(45).** John Paul II warned against certain more educated people disparaging the "ignorant masses"; better knowledge should lead to deeper holiness. **(46).** Saint Francis of Assisi and Saint Anthony of Padua assert that true Christian wisdom can never be separated from mercy toward one's neighbor.

Contemporary Pelagianism (47–48). (47). Gnosticism has given way to the heresy of Pelagianism. **(48).** Pelagianism forgot that all depends on a merciful God, not on human will or human effort. **A Will Lacking Humility (49–51). (49).** Pelagianism asserts that all things are possible through human will and effort. **(50).** Pelagianism minimizes the importance of God's grace and overemphasizes human abilities and strengths. **(51).**

Faith demands that we surrender to God, a loving Father, and stop trying to live our lives without him.

An Often-Overlooked Church Teaching (52–56). (52). The Church repeatedly teaches from the time of the early Church Fathers that we are not justified by our own works or efforts, but by the grace of the Lord. **(53).** Church councils have consistently taught that nothing human can demand, merit, or buy the gift of God's grace. **(54).** The *Catechism of the Catholic Church* reminds us that grace is a gift and we cannot buy it by our works. **(55).** We cannot celebrate the Lord's friendship unless we realize that our earthly life and all our natural abilities are gifts from God. **(56).** Only on the basis of God's gift, freely accepted and humbly received, can we cooperate by our own efforts and contribute to our spiritual transformation.

New Pelagians (57–59). (57). The new Pelagians do not allow themselves to be led by the Spirit in the way of love; they are not passionate about communicating the beauty and joy of the Gospel. **(58).** These people often give excessive importance to certain rules, customs, or ways of acting. **(59).** If one believes that everything depends on human effort, we unconsciously complicate the Gospel and then religion becomes burdensome.

The Summation of the Law (60–62). (60). There is a hierarchy of virtues, and primacy belongs to the theological virtues; Saint Paul asserts that what truly counts is "faith working through love" (Gal 5:6). **(61).** Jesus asks us to see the face of God in the least, the most vulnerable, the defenseless, and those in need. **(62).** We ask the Lord to free the Church (and us) from all new forms of Gnosticism and Pelagianism.

CHAPTER THREE: IN THE LIGHT OF THE MASTER

(63). There are many theories about what constitutes holiness; it is best to turn to Jesus' own words, especially the Sermon on the

Mount. **(64).** In the Beatitudes, "blessed" becomes a synonym for "holy"; through self-giving, one gains true happiness, authentic blessedness. **Going against the Flow (65–66). (65).** We can only truly live the Beatitudes if we are empowered by the Holy Spirit to overcome our weakness, selfishness, complacency, and pride. **(66).** We listen to Jesus' words in the individual Beatitudes of Matthew's Gospel (Mt 5:3–12).

"Blessed are the poor in spirit, for theirs is the kingdom of heaven" (67–70). (67). When one looks deeply into one's heart and asks about the source of security, one realizes it is not found in earthly treasures. **(68).** Wealth ensures nothing; it often blinds us to God's word and the true love of our brothers and sisters. **(69).** Spiritual poverty is closely linked to "holy indifference" (Saint Ignatius of Loyola); it brings radiant interior freedom. **(70).** Saint Luke does not speak of poverty "of spirit," but simply of those who are "poor" (Lk 6:20); we configure ourselves to Jesus who, though rich, "made himself poor" (2 Cor 8:9). *Being poor of heart: that is holiness.*

"Blessed are the meek, for they will inherit the earth" (71–74). (71). Human pride and vanity often make a person think that he or she has the right to dominate others; Jesus proposes the way of meekness, exemplified by his humble entrance to Jerusalem riding on a donkey. **(72).** We strive to regard the faults and limitations of others with meekness; Jesus asks us to learn from him, for he is gentle and humble of heart (Mt 11:29). **(73).** Saint Paul speaks of meekness as one of the fruits of the Holy Spirit (Gal 5:23); this gift should guide everything we do. **(74).** The biblical word *anawim* refers to both the poor and the meek; they will inherit the earth (Mt 5:4). *Reacting with meekness and humility: that is holiness.*

"Blessed are those who mourn, for they will be comforted" (75–76). (75). The world has no desire to mourn or face situations of suffering, yet the cross can never be absent from life. **(76).** One who accepts life's reality compassionately sympathizes with those who suffer. *Knowing how to mourn with others: that is holiness.*

"Blessed are those who hunger and thirst for righteousness, for they will be filled" (77–79). (77). Hunger and thirst are intense human experiences; we ought to desire justice with similar intensity. **(78).** The justice Jesus offers differs from that of the world; we never give up fighting for Gospel justice. **(79).** Justice comes about in people's lives when they themselves always act justly, particularly toward the most vulnerable. *Hungering and thirsting for righteousness: that is holiness.*

"Blessed are the merciful, for they will receive mercy" (80–82). (80). Mercy has two aspects: helping and serving others is coupled with forgiveness and understanding. **(81).** Giving and forgiving demand being merciful "even as your Father is merciful" (Lk 6:36); we will receive mercy in the same measure we give it (Lk 6:38). **(82).** Jesus demands that we forgive—even "seventy times seven" (Mt 18:22). *Seeing and acting with mercy: that is holiness.*

"Blessed are the pure in heart, for they will see God" (83–86). (83). Biblical language uses "heart" to describe our real intentions; our hearts must be pure, simple, and undefiled, for the Lord looks into the heart (1 Sam 16:7). **(84).** We seek to guard our heart from any falsehood, for we know that the Father "sees in secret" (Mt 6:6). **(85).** Matthew reminds us that what proceeds from the heart is that which defiles us (Mt 15:18). **(86).** A heart that loves God and neighbor is a pure heart and can see God. *Keeping a heart free of all that tarnishes love: that is holiness.*

"Blessed are the peacemakers, for they will be called children of God" (87–89). (87). This Beatitude makes us think of endless situations of war in the world; we also think of the destructive nature of gossip. **(88).** Peacemakers truly "make" peace;

they build peace and friendship wherever possible; they actively pursue peace. **(89).** Building authentic evangelical peace is difficult and demanding; it is a craft that demands serenity, creativity, sensitivity, and skill. *Sowing peace all around us: that is holiness.*

"Blessed are those who are persecuted for righteousness' sake, for theirs is the kingdom of heaven" (90–94). (90). Jesus warns us that the path he proposes goes against the flow, challenging us not to long for an easy life. **(91).** The Beatitudes are not easy to live out; one who practices them may be viewed negatively, facing suspicion and ridicule. **(92).** When facing weariness and pain, the cross remains the source of our strength and sanctification. **(93).** As Christians, we hope to be close to people, not aloof; we avoid vanity, negativity, and bitterness. **(94).** Persecutions are not a reality of the past; we experience them today in a variety of forms. *Accepting daily the path of the Gospel, even though it may cause us problems: that is holiness.*

The Great Criterion (95). One clear criterion of authentic holiness is that found in Matthew's narrative of the Last Judgment (Mt 25:31–46): one's action to the least of Jesus' brethren.

In Fidelity to the Master (96–99). (96). Holiness is not about "swooning in mystic rapture"; it means seeing Jesus in the faces of those with whom he himself wished to be identified. **(97).** One necessarily accepts the uncompromising demands of Jesus and practices mercy, "the beating heart of the Gospel." **(98).** Holiness cannot be understood apart from the recognition of the dignity of each human being. **(99).** Holiness also involves seeking social change and the restoration of just social and economic systems.

Ideologies Striking at the Heart of the Gospel (100–103). (100). One harmful error that is contra-Gospel involves separating the Gospel's social demands from one's personal relationship with the Lord. **(101)**. Another error is to be a "one-issue Catholic"; the defense of the unborn must be clear, firm, and passionate, but this concern must be integrated with all aspects of integral justice. **(102)**. Another example would note that the care for migrants is not a secondary issue to complex bioethical questions. **(103)**. Spiritual wisdom includes welcoming the stranger, the hungry, the homeless, and the naked.

The Worship Most Acceptable to God (104–109). (104). Prayer and worship of God are precious and must be integrated with our concern for our brothers and sisters. **(105)**. Holiness is authentic when linked to mercy, the very foundation of the Church's life. **(106)**. Saint Thomas Aquinas affirms that our love of God is best manifested in our mercy toward our neighbor. **(107)**. Saint Teresa of Calcutta asserts that God depends on us to manifest his love for the world. **(108)**. One must be on guard with the use of time and not be consumed in frivolous activities that detract from the service of our neighbor. **(109)**. Frequent reflection on Jesus' words will enable us to better put our Christianity into practice.

CHAPTER FOUR: SIGNS OF HOLINESS IN TODAY'S WORLD

(110). Numerous means of sanctification are already known to us (prayer, sacraments, etc.); however, we can examine certain additional aspects of the call to holiness. **(111)**. These five signs (presented below) are not the sum total of holiness, but they are great expressions of our love of God and neighbor.

Perseverance, Patience, and Meekness (112–121). (112). Holiness begins with a solid grounding in the God who loves and sustains us; faith in God leads us to be faithful to others. **(113)**. We strive to overcome evil with good, not responding with additional evil. **(114)**. We need to recognize and combat our aggressive and selfish inclinations. **(115)**. Christians seek to avoid "verbal violence" in any form, thus offending against the Eighth Commandment. **(116)**. One must always hold one's tongue in regard to the faults of a brother or a sister. **(117)**. Rejoice in the good of others; overcome evil with good; banish the devil; possess a happy heart. **(118)**. The path to holiness requires enduring humiliation in imitation of Jesus. **(119)**. Daily humiliations (sometimes even an injustice) need to be offered to the Lord. **(120)**. One accepts humiliations, knowing this is following in Jesus' footsteps. **(121)**. Acting in this manner presumes a heart set at peace by Christ and freed from egoism.

Joy and a Sense of Humor (122–128). **(122)**. Far from being timid, morose, acerbic, or putting on a dreary face, the saints are joyful and full of good humor. **(123)**. The prophets announced that the times of Jesus would be a revelation of joy. **(124)**. Mary proclaimed, "My spirit rejoices" (Lk 1:47); after Jesus' resurrection the disciples manifested "much joy" (Acts 8:8). **(125)**. Though hard times may come, Christian joy assures deep security, serene hope, and spiritual fulfillment. **(126**. Christian joy is usually accompanied by a sense of humor as seen in the lives of Saints Thomas More, Vincent de Paul, and Philip Neri; ill humor is no sign of holiness. **(127)**. God desires our happiness; we rejoice in simple pleasures following the example of Saint Francis of Assisi. **(128)**. Fraternal love and communion increase our capacity for joy, since they make us capable of rejoicing in the good of others: "Rejoice with those who rejoice" (Rom 12:15).

Boldness and Passion (129–139). **(129)**. Holiness includes boldness (*parrhesia* in Greek), an impulse to evangelize and to leave a mark on this world. **(130)**. Saint Pope Paul VI has spoken about obstacles to evangelization, noting in particular the lack of fervor or boldness. **(131)**. We can look to Jesus to see that boldness and apostolic courage are essential to mission. **(132)**. Boldness is a seal of the Holy Spirit, testifying to the authenticity of one's preaching. **(133)**. The Spirit's promptings are needed, lest one become paralyzed by fear or excessive caution. **(134)**. At times we are like the prophet Jonah, tempted to seek safe havens in many forms. **(135)**. God encourages us to set out anew; if we go to the fringes, we will discover God is already there. **(136)**. Jesus stands at the door and knocks (Rev 3:20); let us open the door of our hearts. **(137)**. Complacency is very seductive and incapacitating; we are tempted to ask: Why even bother? **(138)**. Today's Church needs passionate missionaries, enthusiastic about sharing Christ's life with others. **(139)**. Let us implore the Lord for apostolic courage so as to avoid making our Christian life "a museum of memories!"

In Community (140–146). **(140)**. Living apart from others results in isolation and the loss of our sense of reality and inner clarity. **(141)**. Growth in holiness is a journey in community; this holds true for religious as well as for laypersons. **(142)**. Sharing the Word and Eucharist fosters fraternity and shapes us as a holy, missionary community. **(143)**. The many forms of community (family, parish, religious groups) emerge from small everyday things. **(144)**. Jesus frequently asked his disciples to pay attention to details (lack of wine, a missing sheep, the widow with two coins, etc.). **(145)**. Cherishing the little details of love creates an open and evangelizing environment where the risen Lord is present. **(146)**. In today's environment of consumerist individualism, we seek to follow Jesus' prayer that all may be one (Jn 17:21).

In Constant Prayer (147–157). **(147)**. Holiness consists in habitual openness to the transcendent; there is no holiness without prayer. **(148)**. Saint John of the Cross tells us to always remain in God's presence in all our many activities. **(149)**. Saint Teresa of Avila asserts that silent moments with God are essential; it is then that we hear God's voice. **(150)**. Without listening to the Master, our words are nothing but useless chatter. **(151).** Contemplation restores our humanity; if we are not warmed with God's love and tenderness, we will never catch fire. **(152).** Never should we consider prayerful silence as a form of escape or rejection of the world. **(153).** Reviewing our own history reveals God's abundant mercy (refer to Saint Ignatius of Loyola's "Contemplation for Attaining Love"). **(154).** We employ various forms of prayer (e.g., supplication, intercession, thanksgiving). **(155).** We worship God and live for him, because we are convinced that he exists. **(156).** God's Word has power to transform us; it is both "sweeter than honey" (Ps 119:103) and also a "two-edged sword" (Heb 4:12). **(157).** Meeting Jesus in the Scriptures leads us to the Eucharist.

CHAPTER FIVE: SPIRITUAL COMBAT, VIGILANCE AND DISCERNMENT

(158). The Christian life is a constant battle; we rejoice when the Lord triumphs in our lives. **Combat and Vigilance (159).** Our spiritual battle is not merely against a worldly mentality or human weakness; it is a constant struggle against the devil. **More Than a Myth (160–161). (160).** We cannot deny the existence of the devil or that he is not at work; we pray daily for deliverance from him, the evil one. **(161).** Never think of the devil "as a myth, a representation, a symbol, a figure of speech, or an idea"; he poisons us with "the venom of hatred, desolation, envy, and vice."

Alert and Trustful (162–163). (162). In our spiritual combat, we employ prayer, God's Word, the Eucharist, reconciliation, charity, community life, and missionary outreach. **(163).** Our Christian triumph is always a cross, yet a cross with a victorious banner. **Spiritual Corruption (164–165). (164).** The path of holiness is a source of peace and joy; we seek to avoid lukewarmness. **(165).** We also avoid self-deception and the blindness of comfortable self-satisfaction. **Discernment (166).** Discernment, a gift we implore from the Holy Spirit, enables us to know if something is from the Holy Spirit or from the evil one, the devil.

An Urgent Need (167–168). (167). The gift of discernment is an urgent necessity today; without it we become prey to every passing trend. **(168).** Discernment enables us to evaluate our desires, anxieties, fears, and questions and to discern the "signs of the times." **Always in the Light of the Lord (169).** We employ discernment at all times, engaging in dialogue with the Lord and a sincere daily "examination of conscience."

A Supernatural Gift (170–171). (170). Spiritual discernment does not exclude existential, psychological, sociological, or moral insights from the human sciences, yet we recognize that it is a grace from God. **(171).** Prayer always remains essential to perceive God's voice. **Speak, Lord (172–173). (172).** Prayerful discernment demands readiness to listen to the Lord, to others, and to reality, setting aside one's own partial or insufficient ideas. **(173).** A listening attitude incorporates the Gospel, the Magisterium, and the Discernment of Spirits.

The Logic of the Gift and of the Cross (174–177). (174). Progress in the spiritual life incorporates a growing understanding of God's patience and his timetable; generosity is also required to accomplish the mission one received at Baptism. **(175).** We fully accept the reality: "God asks everything of us, yet he also gives everything to us." **(176).** We constantly turn to Mary, because she lived the Beatitudes of Jesus as none other; we frequently whisper, "Hail Mary…." **(177).** Francis closes his presentation by expressing his hope that his reflections will promote the desire for holiness and result in a deeper happiness.

7

Christus Vivit
Christ Is Alive

(March 25, 2019)

Pope Francis marked the feast of the Annunciation in 2019 by releasing his apostolic exhortation *Christus Vivit* (*Christ Lives*); it is the fruit of listening and discerning during the October 2018 Synod of Bishops, focused on the theme "Young People, the Faith, and Vocational Discernment." The inviting document is presented in nine chapters, roughly corresponding to the pastoral method of "see, judge, act," or, in the framework of the Asian bishops, "dialogue, discernment, deeds." Succinctly presented, the first three chapters present "observations" (scriptural, theological, sociological); the middle three chapters offer an "assessment" (spiritual, developmental, generational); the final three chapters focus on "action" (pastoral, missionary, synodal). Taken together, *Christus Vivit* constitutes a Magna Carta for youth and pastoral ministry.

Several rich themes emerge from a comprehensive review of this lengthy document (127 pages; 299 sections). There is an obvious emphasis on Christ; Francis asserts, "Christ is alive and he wants you to be alive" (1). "In Jesus, all the young can see themselves" (31). The Church should not be "excessively caught up in herself, but instead, and above all, reflect Jesus Christ. This means humbly acknowledging that some things concretely need to change" (39). One finds much emphasis on the theme of communication in society and in the Church, since it impacts "our self-understanding, our understanding of others and the world, and our ability to communicate, learn, be informed, and enter into relationship with others" (86). Francis explores Scripture and the lives of young saints in this pastoral letter, written "with great affection" (3).

Presented in a unique style expressive of closeness, frankness, simplicity, tenderness, and warmth, Pope Francis is eliciting our personal response. With pastoral boldness, Francis is inviting all in the Church to become a serving Church, one that is not silent or afraid to speak to pivotal issues facing the world today; this means fostering a humble community, one that listens, particularly to the insights of the youth. Francis asks all to turn to Mary as "the supreme model for a youthful Church that seeks to follow Christ with enthusiasm and docility" (43). We can only meet these many challenges, if we personally "encounter each day your best friend, the friend who is Jesus" (151). Obviously, Pope Francis is speaking from his heart to our hearts, inviting us to strive to be "open-hearted" missionary-disciples!

Christus Vivit
Synthesis Text

CHRIST IS ALIVE

Introduction (1–4). (1). Christ brings youth to our world, because he is alive and desires us to also be alive. **(2).** Christ is in us to restore our strength and hope, especially when we feel we are growing old due to sorrow, resentment or fear, doubt or failure. **(3).** Pope Francis addresses young people to encourage them; he sends the same message to the entire People of God. **(4).** Francis is drawing many of his insights from the Church's synodal journey on youth from 2016 to 2019.

CHAPTER ONE: WHAT DOES THE WORD OF GOD HAVE TO SAY ABOUT YOUNG PEOPLE?

(5). We can draw on Sacred Scripture for it often speaks about young people and how the Lord draws near to encounter them.

In the Old Testament (6–11). (6). Though not highly regarded, the young Joseph outshone all his brothers in important affairs (Gen 37–47). **(7).** Gideon was ordered by God to go and deliver Israel (Jg 6:13–14). **(8).** Samuel was still a young boy when the Lord spoke to him, and he responded to God's call: "Speak, Lord, for your servant is listening" (1 Sam 3:9–10). King Saul was young when given a mission by the Lord (1 Sam 9:2). **(9).** King David is chosen, for the Lord sees into people's hearts (1 Sam 16:6–13). **(10).** Solomon, though a mere youth (1 Kg 3:7), asks God for wisdom when he is chosen. Jeremiah shows what can happen when the brashness of youth is joined to God's power (Jer 1:6–8). **(11).** The Jewish servant girl of Naaman helps him get cured (2 Kgs 5:2–5). The young Ruth is a model of generosity and faithfulness (Ru 4:1–17).

In the New Testament (12–21). (12). In one of Jesus' parables (Lk 15:11–32) the younger son, though he had made a mistake, has the courage to start anew, while the older son had a hardened heart. **(13).** Jesus desires to give us young hearts. Saint Paul encourages us to have youthful hearts that are capable of loving (Col 3:9–14). **(14).** Jesus asks that the greatest must become like the youngest (Lk 22:26). **(15).** Young people should be treated as brothers and given encouragement. Pope Francis constantly urges young people "not to let themselves be robbed of hope" (cf. 1 Tim 4:12).

(16). A wise young person is open to learning from other's experience. **(17).** Mark the Evangelist (cf. 10:17–22) notes how a rich young man allowed the passing years to rob his dreams, preferring attachment to his riches. **(18)**. Matthew's Gospel (19:16–22) portrays a young man who had surrendered his youth to riches and comforts. **(19)**. The Gospels compare the wise and foolish young women (Mt 25:1–13). **(20)**. Jesus encourages anyone who has lost his inner vitality, dreams, enthusiasm, optimism, or generosity to arise to renewed life (Lk 7:14). **(21)**. Numerous other biblical passages shed light on the time of youth as a pivotal stage of life.

Chapter Two: Jesus, Ever Young

(22). The synod spoke some insightful words, saying, "youth is an original and stimulating stage of life, which Jesus himself experienced, thereby sanctifying it."

Jesus' Youth (23–29). (23). Jesus gave his life for us when he was, in today's terms, a young adult. **(24)**. The Gospels tell us nothing about Jesus' childhood; however, it recounts some events of his adolescence and youth (refugee in Egypt, repatriation in Nazareth). **(25)**. Jesus' Baptism is a consecration as he embarks on his life's mission. The Father says, "You are my beloved child"; every young person is invited to hear those same words. **(26)**. As an adolescent Jesus went with his parents to the temple in Jerusalem, after which he returned dutifully to Nazareth. **(27)**. The years of Jesus' youth set him on the path of his sublime mission. **(28)**. Jesus fully shared in the life of his family and people, even learning his father's carpenter trade (Mt 13:55; Mk 6:3). **(29)**. Clearly, Jesus readily interacted with his wider family, friends, and relatives, journeying with this broader community to Jerusalem (Lk 2:41–45).

His Youth Teaches Us (30–33). (30). Inspired by Jesus' experience, the Church needs projects that strengthen young people to generously engage in service and mission. **(31)**. Much can be learned from Jesus: trust in the Father, compassion for the weakest, the experience of being misunderstood, the fear of suffering. **(32).** The risen Jesus wants to make us sharers in the new life of resurrection, keeping alive all our dreams, projects, and ideals. Recall the young man at the empty tomb who tells the women not to be afraid and to proclaim the joy of the resurrection (Mk 16:6–7). **(33).** Jesus invites the youth "to enkindle stars in the night of other young people," recalling that he is the "bright morning star" (Rev 22:16).

The Youth of the Church (34). Youth, more than simply a period of time, is a state of mind. The Church is called to return with all her heart to her first love. This invitation was reiterated at the Second Vatican Council in its message to the young: "The Church is the real youth of the world."

A Church Open to Renewal (35–38). (35). We are to ask the Lord to free the Church from those who wish to make her grow old. She best shows her youth when she returns to her source. **(36).** Though not standing apart from people, the Church dares to be different, pointing to ideals such as generosity, service, purity, forgiveness, prayer, and several others. **(37).** If the Church is tempted to lose enthusiasm, she can turn to young people to help keep her young. **(38).** Those in the Church who are no longer young need to find ways to remain close to the voices and concerns of young people, thus making the Church a place of dialogue and fraternity.

A Church Attentive to the Signs of the Times (39–42). (39). Though the Church may seem empty to the young, still they are sensitive to Jesus when he is presented in an attractive way. The Church needs to appreciate both the vision and the criticisms of young people. **(40).** The synod acknowledged that a substantial number of young people do not find the Church significant for them; admittedly, there are serious and understandable reasons for this reaction. **(41).** To be credible to young people, there are times that the Church must regain her humility and simply listen; she needs to understand and preach the Gospel with greater depth. **(42)**. A living Church must be "attentive to the legitimate claims of those women who seek greater justice and equality."

Mary, the Young Woman of Nazareth (43–48). **(43)**. Mary is the supreme model for a youthful Church that seeks to follow Christ with enthusiasm and docility (see Lk 1:38). **(44)**. We should be struck by the strength of Mary's "yes"; she was committed, willing to take a great risk. Her yes and her desire to serve were stronger than any doubts or difficulties. **(45)**. Mary accompanied the suffering of her Son without evasions or illusions; from her we can learn how to say yes with stubborn endurance and creativity. **(46)**. Mary was a young woman whose heart overflowed with joy (see Lk 1:47); she was energetic, going with haste to serve her cousin Elizabeth (Lk 1:39). **(47)**. When the family was in danger, she set out with Joseph to a distant land (Mt 2:13–14); she joined the disciples awaiting the outpouring of the Holy Spirit (Acts 1:14). **(48)**. Today, Mother Mary watches over us her children on our life's journey. She loves the Church, a youthful, pilgrim people. "Thus, Mary illumines anew our youth."

Young Saints (49–63). **(49)**. The Church is full of young saints who devoted their lives to Christ, many even suffering martyrdom. **(50)**. Through the holiness of the young, the Church can renew her spiritual ardor and apostolic vigor; numerous examples exist. **(51)**. Sebastian tried to convert his soldier companions; ordered to renounce his faith, he chose a martyr's death. **(52)**. Francis of Assisi embraced poverty and sought to rebuild the Church, dying in 1226. **(53)**. Joan of Arc, a young peasant girl, fought to defend France from invaders. **(54)**. Blessed Andrew Phu Yen, a seventeenth-century Vietnamese catechist, was imprisoned and martyred. **(55)**. Saint Kateri Tekakwitha, a

North American native, died saying, "Jesus, I love you." **(56)**. Saint Dominic Savio sought to live his faith with constant joy, dying at age fourteen.

(57). Saint Therese of the Child Jesus lived her "little way" of complete trust in the Lord. **(58)**. Blessed Ceferino Namuncura, an Argentinian, sought to bring the faith to his indigenous tribe. **(59)**. Blessed Isidore Bakanja, a layman from the Congo, witnessed to his faith, forgiving his executioner. **(60)**. Blessed Pier Giorgio Frassati sought to return Jesus' love by helping the poor. **(61)**. Blessed Marcel Callo died in a concentration camp in Austria, always seeking to strengthen his fellow prisoners. **(62)**. Blessed Chiara Badano, who died in 1990, experienced how pain can be transformed by love. **(63)**. Hopefully, these young people, who lived the Gospel to the full, may attract many joyous, courageous, and committed young people to the Church to offer the world new testimonies of holiness!

CHAPTER THREE: YOU ARE THE "NOW" OF GOD

(64). Young people are not only the future, they are the "now" of our world; we need to sincerely ask, "What are today's young people really like? What is going on in their lives?"

In Positive Terms (65–67). **(65)**. The Church seeks to set aside narrow preconceptions and to listen carefully to the young; this empathy enriches her, enabling her to appreciate new sensitivities and to consider new questions. **(66)**. If adults list the problems and failings of today's young people, this attitude will create greater distance and less closeness. **(67)**. We need a farsightedness that enables discernment of new pathways; each person's heart should be considered "holy ground" before which we must "take off our shoes."

Many Ways of Being Young (68–70). **(68)**. The world's youth is not a homogeneous group; today many distinct groups with varied experiences exist in different regions around the world. **(69)**.

Demographically, some regions have a low birth rate, while others are high. Some areas are influenced by Christian traditions; others are marked by diverse religious backgrounds. There is religious persecution in some places. **(70).** The synod sought to recognize these divergences, while also seeking to appreciate the contributions that diversity brings. **Some Experiences of Young People (71).** It is beneficial to realize that "youth" does not exist; there are only young people with a great diversity in today's rapidly changing world.

Living in a World in Crisis (72–80). (72). Many young people today live in very unsettled situations, taking countless forms: war, extortion, organized crime, human trafficking, and so forth; such violence destroys many young lives. **(73).** Others may be taken in by ideologies or even become individualists. **(74).** There are other forms of marginalization and social exclusion for religious, ethnic, or economic reasons; women are doubly impacted by such situations. **(75).** As a Church, may we never fail to weep before the tragedies of our young. **(76).** "Some realities in life are only seen with eyes cleansed by tears." We ask ourselves: Can I weep? "Weeping is also an expression of mercy and compassion." **(77).** Some pain is so deep that one can only tell God how much one is suffering. Recall Jesus' words: "Blessed are those who mourn, for they shall be comforted" (Mt 5:4). **(78).** When ideological colonization happens, this is especially harmful to the young; they often end being discarded in a "throwaway culture." **(79).** Modern culture often exploits the image of the young. **(80).** Generational conflicts between the young and adults prove harmful.

Desires, Hurts, and Longings (81–85). (81). Young people, aware that the body and sexuality have importance for their lives, seek a healthy interrelationship that emerges from open discussion. **(82).** While biomedical technologies have influenced perceptions about the body, we must never forget that life is a gift. **(83).** When the young experience setbacks, disappointments, and profoundly painful memories, they can recall that Jesus makes his presence felt amid these crosses. **(84).** The Church recognizes that young people feel a desire for God, although it may be still vague and far from knowledge of the God of revelation. **(85).** Three areas of importance were discussed by the synod: (a) the digital environment, (b) migrants, and (c) forms of abuse.

The Digital Environment (86–90). (86). We live in a highly digitalized culture that has a profound impact on ideas of time and space, our understanding of others, and our ability to communicate. **(87).** The Web and social networks have created new ways to communicate and bond; they become a public square where young people spend much of their time. **(88).** These realities also have limitations and deficiencies; it is not healthy to confuse authentic communication with mere virtual contact. **(89).** One must not forget that there are huge economic interests operating in the digital world; there is also the proliferation of fake news. **(90).** Young people themselves have pointed out that "online relationships can become inhuman" and that inappropriate use of technology "creates a delusional parallel reality that ignores human dignity." Helpful ways need to be found "to pass from virtual contact to good and healthy communication."

Migrants as an Epitome of Our Time (91–94). (91). The Church has deep concern for migrants, especially those fleeing from war, violence, and political or religious persecution. **(92).** Some migrants are attracted by Western culture and develop unrealistic expectations; others fall victim to traffickers of various kinds. Some will meet a xenophobic reaction. **(93).** Young migrants often experience separation from their place of origin, as well as cultural and religious uprooting. **(94).** The Church is challenged to provide a welcoming presence to migrants, a supportive community.

Ending Every Form of Abuse (95–102). **(95).** Abuse of various kinds is widespread in society and it also affects the Church. **(96).** The scourge of the sexual abuse of minors is a phenomenon in all cultures and societies; it "is in no way less monstrous when it takes place within the Church." **(97).** The Church needs to adopt rigorous preventative measures intended to avoid the recurrence of such crimes. **(98).** Abuses exist in a variety of forms: abuse of power or conscience, sexual and financial abuse. The Church recognizes that clericalism is a constant temptation on the part of priests.

(99). The Church appreciates all those who have the courage to report any evil they experience in the Church; she also lauds the generous commitment of countless persons in the Church, especially those dedicated to the service of the young. **(100).** Statistics show that those who commit crimes are not the majority of priests; most serve with fidelity and generosity. All are asked to speak to the proper authorities if they see a priest who is at risk. **(101).** Clearly, the pilgrim Church shares "the joys and hope, the grief and anguish" (GS 1) of all humanity. **(102).** In the midst of these various tragedies, the Church finds an opportunity for genuine reform.

A Way Out (103–110). **(103).** This chapter has looked at the reality of young people today; it does not claim to be exhaustive; it seeks to provide pastoral care. **(104).** Even in dark moments, there is a way out, exemplified by Venerable Carlo Acutis. **(105).** Carlo knew how to use new communications technology to transmit the Gospel message. **(106).** Carlo did not fall into the trap of consumerism and distraction; he maintained his originality. **(107).** Do not be robbed of hope and joy; do not be a photocopy, be an original! **(108).** One's youthful years serve an important purpose, if one fills them with generous commitments, dedication, and even difficult sacrifices. **(109).** When one feels weak, weary, or disillusioned, ask Jesus to renew you; with him, hope never fails. **(110).** It is essential to live with others, for in unity one finds marvelous strength.

CHAPTER FOUR: A GREAT MESSAGE FOR ALL YOUNG PEOPLE

(111). Pope Francis says he wants to speak directly to young people about three great truths: (a) God is Love, (b) Christ saves us, and (c) Jesus is alive.

A God Who Is Love (112–117). **(112).** Truly, God loves us; we should never doubt this truth. **(113).** Though one's experience of fatherhood may have its limitations, each one can find security in the embrace of the heavenly Father. **(114).** Many expressions of God's love are found in the Scriptures. Some examples are Hosea 11:4 [I was to them like those who lift infants to their cheeks]; Isaiah 49:6, 15; 43:4; Zephaniah 3:17; Jeremiah 31:3 [I have loved you with an everlasting love]. **(115).** Let us recall that God's memory "is a heart filled with tender compassion"; rest in this loving embrace. **(116).** God's love is a daily, discreet, and respectful love, a love that heals and raises up. **(117).** When God asks something, make room for him to push you and to help you grow. Seek God's closeness in the loving face of his courageous witnesses here on earth.

Christ Saves You (118–123). **(118).** Another great truth is that Christ, out of love, sacrificed himself completely in order to save us personally (cf. Jn 13:1; Gal 2:20). **(119).** Look to Christ's cross, cling to him, let him save you. Never forget he forgives us seventy times seven, all with a tenderness that never disappoints. **(120).** The Lord's love is greater than all our problems, frailties, and flaws; he embraced the prodigal son, also Peter after his denials. **(121).** God's forgiveness and salvation are not something we can buy; we can only receive them with immense gratitude. **(122).** Young people, how valuable you are, since you were redeemed by the precious blood of

Christ; you are priceless! **(123)**. Keep your eyes on the outstretched arms of Christ crucified.

He Is Alive! (124–129). **(124)**. The third truth, inseparable from the second, is that Christ is alive; he is not just a distant memory. **(125)**. Since he lives, he can be present in our lives at every moment. **(126)**. Let us rejoice with Christ as a friend who loves us and desires to triumph in us. **(127)**. Since Jesus is eternally alive, we will also have life if we cling to him. **(128)**. With him our hearts experience a security that is firmly rooted and enduring. **(129)**. If we let Jesus love and save us, we will have a profound experience capable of sustaining our entire Christian life.

The Spirit Gives Life (130–133). **(130)**. In all the three truths presented in this chapter, we encounter God the Father and Jesus; in addition, the Holy Spirit flows over into our lives. **(131)**. We daily ask the Spirit's assistance; in this we will find genuine happiness. **(132)**. Discover that beautiful poem often attributed to Father Pedro Arrupe, titled "Fall in Love." Its first line is, "Nothing is more practical than finding God, than falling in love in a quite absolute, final way." Note: This poem is readily available on the internet. **(133)**. God is the true source of youth at its best; we can walk and not grow weary or faint (see Is 40:30–31).

Chapter Five: Paths of Youth

(134–135). **(134)**. Pope Francis personally addresses the youth, asserting that to be young is a grace, a blessing, a gift of God. **(135)**. God is the giver of youth, a season of life, worthwhile in itself, not just a brief prelude to adulthood.

A Time of Dreams and Decisions (136–143). **(136)**. In Jesus' day, the passage from childhood was a significant step in life. **(137)**. Youth, a stage in personality development, is marked by dreams, relationships, trials, experiments, and choices, all building one's life project. **(138)**. God's love does not stifle our dreams. There is a healthy restlessness; Saint Augustine noted, "You have made us for yourself, Lord, and our hearts are restless until they find their rest in you." **(139)**. To talk about young people is to talk about promise and to talk about joy.

(140). Youth is not stagnant; young people make decisions in professional, social, and political fields, and also about love, choosing a spouse, and starting a family. **(141)**. It is useless to complain or give up. Remember that Jesus is the way; "welcome him into your 'boat' and put out into the deep." **(142)**. Keep following your hopes and dreams. If mistakes are made, get up and start over; no one has the right to rob you of hope. **(143)**. Young people, make the most of your youthful years. "Do not become the sorry sight of an abandoned vehicle." "Make a ruckus! Cast out the fears that paralyze you, so that you don't become young mummies!"

A Thirst for Life and Experience (144–149). **(144)**. Always make the most of the opportunities life offers. **(145)**. Contrary to what many may think, the Lord does not want to stifle one's desires for a fulfilling life. **(146)**. With open eyes, we are to experience fully and with gratitude every one of life's little gifts. **(147)**. Enjoy the present; do not worry about tomorrow; make the most of life's little joys as gifts of God's love. **(148)**. The imprisoned Cardinal Francis Nguyen Van Thuan sought to live each day as enthusiastically and fully as possible. **(149)**. Paradoxically, for many Christians, suffering and darkness have become places of encounter with God. Remember that people with physical, mental, and sensory disabilities have gifts to give.

In Friendship with Christ (150–157). **(150)**. One will only know the fullest meaning of youth through an encounter with Jesus, "your best friend." **(151)**. Friendship is one of life's gifts; faithful friends are also a reflection of the Lord's love. "There is nothing so precious as a faithful friend" (Sir 6:15). **(152)**. Friendship is meant to be stable, firm, and faithful, maturing with the passage of time. **(153)**. Friendship is so important that Jesus calls himself a friend: "I do not call you servants any longer, but I call you friends" (Jn 15:15). **(154)**. Friendship with Jesus perdures; even if we stray away, "he remains faithful, for he cannot deny himself" (2 Tim 2:13). **(155)**. We can speak and share our deepest secrets with a friend; prayer as conversation with a friend is both a challenge and an adventure. **(156)**. Primarily, Christianity "is a person who loved me immensely, who demands and asks for my love. Christianity is Christ." **(157)**. Jesus can bring all young people of the Church together in a single dream, a dream for which he gave his life on the cross.

Growth in Maturity (158–162). (158). Several elements make young hearts strong: seeking the Lord, keeping his word, entrusting one's life to God, and growing in the virtues. **(159).** Growing spiritually does not mean losing one's spontaneity, boldness, enthusiasm, and tenderness. **(160).** Pope Francis admits that when chosen as pope the Lord gave him a gift of renewed youth. **(161).** Growing older means preserving and cherishing many precious things from our youth. **(162).** In our journey, one needs to discover one's unique pathway of holiness. Saint John of the Cross noted how God wishes to manifest his grace "to some in one way and to others in another" (*Spiritual Canticle*).

Paths of Fraternity (163–167). (163). Spiritual growth is expressed above all by growth in fraternal, generous, and merciful love. **(164).** It is always better to live the faith together; everything becomes easier when done in harmony with others. **(165).** Though hurts and disappointments do come, we never stop trying to listen to God's call to forgiveness. **(166).** At times when our youthful energy, dreams, and enthusiasm may lag, we try to avoid turning inward and focusing on ourselves. **(167).** God loves the joy of young people. Fraternal love multiplies our ability to experience joy. An African proverb says, "If you want to go fast, go alone. If you want to go far, go together."

Young and Committed (168–174). (168). The lay vocation moves outside the Church to charity within the family and to social and political areas, seeking to extend God's Kingdom in this world. **(169).** Youth are called to find ways of building social friendship, avoiding all forms of enmity and promoting "the culture of encounter." **(170).** A specific feature of today's youth is to engage in social commitment and direct contact with the poor. **(171).** All grow in wisdom and maturity when they take time to touch the suffering of others; opportunities are multiple. Such engagement deepens one's faith and often serves for the discernment of one's life vocation. **(172).** Various youth activities often involve young people of other churches and other living religions. **(173).** Though immense and difficult challenges exist, Jesus takes every small effort and multiplies it (see Jn 6:4–13). **(174).** Pope Francis encourages youth involvement, asking them to take to the streets and be protagonists of change. "Dear young people, please, do not be bystanders in life."

Courageous Missioners (175–178). (175). The love of Christ calls young people to be witnesses of the Gospel, fully living their faith. **(176).** While we are witnesses, we also speak about the person of Jesus. Saint Paul notes, "Woe to me if I do not proclaim the Gospel" (1 Cor 9:16). **(177).** There are no limits to where Jesus sends us to be "fearless missionaries"; he counts on the courage, boldness, and enthusiasm of the youth. **(178).** Truly, youth is not an "in-between time." As youth, "you are the now of God, and he wants you to bear fruit!"

CHAPTER SIX: YOUNG PEOPLE WITH ROOTS

(179). Strong trees can withstand storms, because they have strong roots; no one can build a secure future without being firmly grounded.

Don't Allow Yourselves to Be Uprooted (180–186).

(180). Being uprooted is a critical issue on which Pope Francis wishes to offer his reflections. **(181).** If one ignores personal history and past experiences, one will become shallow, uprooted, and distrustful. Ideologies try to deconstruct history; they have a disregard for past history and its spiritual and human riches. **(182).** Beware of those masters of manipulation and their emphasis on "the cult of youth." **(183).** Do not allow them to exploit your youth and promote a shallow life that confuses true beauty with appearances. The springtime of courtship will pass; see the beauty in the fidelity of elderly couples. **(184).** Some false cults promote a spirituality without God, without community or concern for those who suffer; they will enslave you! **(185).** Be alert to aspects of globalization that bring forms of cultural colonialization that sever young people from their cultural and religious roots. **(186).** Care for your roots; they are your source of strength needed to make you grow, flourish, and bear fruit.

Your Relationship with the Elderly (187–191).

(187). It is a genuine act of love to help young people discover the living richness of the past and to treasure its memory. **(188).** When we examine the long years the elderly have lived together and all their life experiences, we look at them with deep respect. **(189).** The commandment to honor one's father and mother retains all its validity. **(190).** Young people can combine a critical spirit with wisdom from past generations. **(191).** The world has never benefitted, nor will it ever benefit, from a rupture between generations.

Dreams and Visions (192–197). (192). When both young and old are open to the Holy Spirit, they make a wonderful combination. **(193).** The elderly have a reservoir of dreams emerging from their experience; without this treasury, young people lose their clear sight of the horizon. **(194).** We seek to keep our elder's dream of a better future alive so as to pass it on to the next generation. **(195).** It is a very good thing to let older people tell their long stories; they are often full of rich experiences, eloquent symbols, and hidden messages. We are prepared to listen patiently. **(196).** The elders serve the special role as "memory keepers." **(197).** Elders teach the young that a life without love is an arid life, and that there is more joy in giving than in receiving.

Taking Risks Together (198–201). (198). A love that acts and takes risks may at times make mistakes. It is most beneficial to view life as a tapestry. The underside may look messy with its tangled threads, but the top side displays a magnificent story! God creates something beautiful—even out of our mistakes! **(199).** In our common journey, young and old learn much from each other, warming hearts and inspiring minds. **(200).** Roots do not chain us to the past; rather they are fixed points from which we grow and meet new challenges. **(201).** Employing an image from the Samoan Islands, the Church can be viewed as a canoe where the elderly keep it on course by judging its position from the stars, while the young keep it moving forward by their rowing.

CHAPTER SEVEN: YOUTH MINISTRY

(202). Youth ministry has been significantly affected by social and cultural changes. Effective approaches must involve the entire community, and young people themselves must play an active role.

A Pastoral Care That Is Synodal (203–208). (203). Young people themselves are the agents of youth ministry, using their insight, ingenuity, and knowledge to approach other youth. **(204).** New styles and flexible strategies must incorporate opportunities for learning, conversing, celebrating, singing, and sharing real-life faith experiences. **(205).** Yet effective practices that have borne fruit and communicate the joy of the Gospel will continue to be employed. **(206).** Youth ministry has to be synodal, involving a "journeying together" that moves toward a participatory and co-responsible Church. **(207).** We can discover that the Church's unity is not monolithic, but rather a network of varied, Spirit-given gifts. **(208).** Let us explore several concrete approaches for renewing youth ministry that emerged from the synod.

Main Courses of Action (209–215). (209). Clearly, youth ministry involves two main courses of action: *outreach* and *growth*. **(210).** As for *outreach*, young people themselves know how to find appealing ways to come together, including effective ways to use social media for evangelization; they need to be encouraged and given freedom to explore ways to reach the hearts of other young people. **(211).** In all outreach programs, the language of closeness must be used; it can touch people's hearts—especially if it is spoken by someone who radiates life. **(212).** As for *growth*, it must be emphasized that the best follow-up to one's initial experience of God's love is ongoing experiences that sustain the Christian life (not doctrinal and moral formation sessions).

(213). Continuing growth will necessarily have two main goals: ongoing kerygmatic formation and concrete experiences in fraternal love, community life, and service. **(214).** Youth ministry should always include opportunities for renewing and deepening of one's personal experience of God's love; such joyful encounters "should never be replaced by a kind of 'indoctrination.'" **(215).** Fraternal love is the "new commandment" (Jn 13:34); showing one's love for God must have a primary place in every project of youth formation.

Suitable Environments (216–220). **(216).** The Church needs to make all her institutions and apostolates more welcoming to young people. **(217).** In a word, this means creating "homes" and "families" where young people feel connected and loved. **(218).** Young people need places that they can make their own, freely coming and going, feeling welcomed, and readily meeting other people. **(219).** Friendship and discussion offer opportunities to strengthen social and relational skills. **(220).** While youth centers are open and free, they should not become isolated and lose all contact with parish communities and movements.

Youth Ministry in Educational Institutions (221–223). **(221).** Schools are important platforms for drawing close to the young. They are in urgent need of self-criticism, so as to better serve the youth in praying and in practicing their faith in the real world. **(222).** Catholic schools remain essential places for the evangelization of the young; however, they need to be renewed and have a revival of missionary outreach. How can they better integrate the knowledge of head, heart, and hands? **(223).** Spiritual and cultural formation go hand-in-hand; all education must be both human and humanizing. Youth programs need to respond to the crippling effects of "cultural consumerism."

Areas Needing to Be Developed (224–229). **(224).** Many young people have come to appreciate silence, closeness to God, and contemplative prayer; they also desire "fresh, authentic, and joyful liturgy." **(225).** Christian service is a unique opportunity for growth in openness to God's gifts of faith and charity. **(226).** The arts (theatre, painting, music) are also a pastoral resource. Saint Augustine says, "Sing, but continue on your journey." **(227).** Sports appeal to young people; they have great potential for education and formation. **(228).** Nature holds special attraction for many adolescents and youth; the spirit of Saint Francis of Assisi opens people to universal fraternity. **(229).** Even in today's challenging times, there are gifts of God that never grow old (the Word, Eucharist, Reconciliation, the witness of saints and spiritual masters).

A "Popular" Youth Ministry (230–238). (230). In addition to ordinary pastoral approaches, there is room for "popular" youth ministry with a different style, schedule, pace, and method. **(231).** Popular leaders are able to make everyone, including the poor, the vulnerable, and the frail and wounded, feel part of a forward-looking youth movement. **(232).** Young people from outside Christian families and institutions often help everyone to see the goodness in others. **(233).** It is important to train the youth to take up their responsibilities, knowing that life's difficulties actually strengthen their humanity. **(234).** Youth ministry should have room for all kinds of young people, showing that we are a Church with open doors.

(235). Room should be available for those who have other visions of life, belong to other religions or to no religion. "All the young, without exception, are in God's heart and thus in the Church's heart." **(236).** Youth ministry is a process that is gradual, respectful, patient, hopeful, tireless, and compassionate. **(237).** The Emmaus encounter (Lk 24:13–35) can serve as a model where Jesus accompanies his struggling disciples; he helps them *recognize* their experience, *interpret* their realities, and *choose* their path of discipleship. **(238).** Popular piety, especially pilgrimages, often attract the young; it is "a legitimate way of living the faith" as noted in *Evangelii Gaudium* 122–126.

Always Missionaries (239–241). (239). A "popular" youth ministry easily moves toward a "popular" missionary activity. **(240).** A closer look reveals that youth ministry is always missionary, enabling youth to look beyond their family or group of friends; it leads to a renewed experience of faith and even serious thoughts about a vocation. **(241).** Young people easily find new fields for mission (e.g., social networks).

Accompaniment by Adults (242–247). (242). Young people need to have their freedom respected, yet they also need accompaniment. **(243).** An accompanying community is important, but it must avoid judging the youth or demanding of them a perfection beyond their years. **(244).** The synod recognized the shortage of qualified people devoted to accompaniment. **(245).** Young people showing leadership potential need accompaniment and formation; seminarians and religious need even greater abilities in this area. **(246).** Young people themselves beautifully described the qualities needed in mentors (about a dozen are noted in the full document). A mentor must believe wholeheartedly in a young person's abilities. **(247).** Church educational institutions must seek to welcome all young people with all their uniqueness and diversity.

CHAPTER EIGHT: VOCATION

(248–249). (248). The word "vocation" broadly means a calling from God, including the call to life, friendship, holiness, and a relationship with God. **(249).** Pope Francis recalls that in *Gaudete et Exsultate* (2) he reproposed "the call to holiness in a practical way for our own time."

God's Call to Friendship (250–252). (250). Jesus wants to be a friend to every young person. Peter's mission to shepherd the Church emerges from Jesus' gratuitous love of friendship. **(251).** The Gospel narrates the sad story of the rich young man who failed to perceive Jesus' gaze of love (cf. Mk 10:21; Mt 19:22). **(252).** God offers us a salvation that is "an invitation to be part of a love story" that is interwoven with our personal stories.

Being There for Others (253–258). (253). Speaking of vocation in the strict sense, it is "a call to missionary service of others." **(254)**. This vocation is linked to service. In *Evangelii Gaudium* (273) Francis spoke of one's self-awareness: "I am a mission on this earth; that is the reason why I am here in this world." **(255)**. One's vocation is expressed in one's work, though vocation is much more. **(256)**. This recognition gives greater value to everything one does and provides a direction in life. **(257)**. To respond to our vocation, we need to foster and develop all that we are, becoming fully aware of the course we are taking. **(258)**. For the youth this "being there for others" normally involves two basic issues: forming a family and working; we examine each one.

Love and Family (259–267). (259). Young people feel the call to love; they dream of meeting the right person with whom they can form a family and build a common life. This theme is treated more extensively in *Amoris Laetitia*. **(260)**. Christians who marry recognize the Lord's call in their own love story; it is an invitation to form one flesh and one life. **(261)**. We recall that God created us as sexual beings; sexuality is a gift from God with two purposes: to love and to generate life. **(262)**. Family continues to be the reference point for young people, even though various pressures are present. We cannot forget that grandparents play a crucial role in affection and religious education.

(263). Though family difficulties exist, it is worth every effort to invest in a family. Francis asserts, "Don't let yourselves be robbed of a great love." **(264)**. Putting aside numerous challenges, Francis urges young people to opt for marriage. **(265)**. Marriage requires preparation; it calls for growth in self-knowledge and a maturing in one's own sexuality. **(266)**. While spouses have weaknesses, they can progressively achieve their ideal of married life in accordance with God's plan. **(267)**. For those who do not marry or do not enter religious life, they (and all Christians) should remember their important vocation received in Baptism.

Work (268–273). (268). Work defines and influences a young adult's identity; it is a prime place where friendships develop. Work allows the young to meet their practical needs and to seek meaning and fulfillment of their dreams. **(269).** Work is a necessity, a path to growth, human development, and personality fulfillment (cf. *Laudato Sí* 125, 128). **(270).** Youth unemployment and other forms of marginalization negatively impact young people's capacity to dream and to hope. **(271).** Work realities form a complex social issue affecting human dignity, development, and social inclusion. **(272).** In spite of the harsh realities of the job market, youth should never give up on their dreams or accept defeat. **(273).** When one realizes that God is calling, one is able to summon up capacities for sacrifice, generosity, and dedication.

The Vocation to Special Consecration (274–277). (274). We are convinced that the Holy Spirit continues to inspire vocations to the priesthood and religious life. **(275).** We believe that the Lord cannot fail in his promise to provide the Church with shepherds. **(276).** Francis asks the youth not to dismiss the possibility that God is calling them to a special vocation within the Church. **(277).** Jesus continues to walk in our midst; leave room for that interior silence where one can perceive Jesus' gaze and hear his call.

CHAPTER NINE: DISCERNMENT

278–282. (278). Though discernment was already discussed in *Gaudete et Exsultate*, Pope Francis now builds on those reflections and applies them to vocational discernment. **(279).** Young people today are bombarded with an endless number of items calling for their attention; without the wisdom of discernment, they can become prey to every passing trend or fad. **(280).** True discernment, while including reason and prudence, seeks to glimpse that unique plan God has for each person. **(281).** Formation of conscience is important for it allows discernment to grow in depth and in fidelity to God. **(282).** In addition, this process of formation helps one grow in the virtue of prudence, giving overall direction to one's life through concrete choices.

Discerning Your Vocation (283–286). (283). One unique form of discernment involves the effort to discover one's personal vocation; this requires a certain degree of solitude and silence as well as prolonged prayer. **(284).** This silence does not make us close in on ourselves. Only when we are prepared to listen do we have the freedom to recognize that God may be offering us something more. **(285).** In discerning one's vocation, there are certain questions we ought to ask. Francis lists eight probing questions; they revolve around self-knowledge and one's place in the Church and society. **(286).** These questions are less centered on ourselves. Rather than continually asking, "Who am I?" the real question is, "For whom am I?" We are for God and for others.

The Call of Jesus Our Friend (287–290). (287). To discern our personal vocation, we have to realize that it is a calling from our friend Jesus. We can use the model of friendship in trying to discover God's will for our lives. **(288).** The Lord sees us as his friend; thus, he desires to give us a grace, a charism, a gift that will perfectly fit us as a unique individual. **(289).** A vocation, while a gift, will undoubtedly also be demanding; one needs to be ready to take risks. **(290).** Succinctly stated: the choice that Jesus sets before us is to follow him in unconditional friendship.

Listening and Accompaniment (291–298). (291). Persons who can help young people with their vocational discernment need the ability to listen; this calls for three distinct and complementary kinds of sensitivity. **(292).** The first kind of sensitivity is directed to *the individual.* The other person must sense that one is listening unconditionally; attentive and selfless listening is a sign of respect for the other person. **(293).** The second kind of sensitivity is marked by *discernment*. It means seeking to understand what the other person is trying to express and to appreciate what is happening in their life; it also includes helping the other person distinguish truth from illusions. **(294).** The third kind of sensitivity is the ability to *perceive what is driving* the other person, helping him or her to see what is most pleasing to the Lord—all from the perspective of the deeper inclinations of the heart.

(295). Thus, discernment is helping the person to follow the Lord more faithfully. **(296).** When we listen in this way, we disappear and allow the other person to follow the path he or she has discovered. **(297).** There are no easy recipes; the important thing is to encourage and accompany others, without ever imposing our own roadmaps. **(298).** If we hope to accompany others on this path, we must be the first to follow it; in this journey we seek to imitate Mary. We implore her maternal presence.

And to Conclude ... A Wish (299). Francis writes, "Dear young people, my joyful hope is to see you keep running the race before you.... Keep running, attracted by the face of Christ, whom we love so much.... May the Holy Spirit urge you on as you run this race.... And when you arrive where we have not yet reached, have the patience to wait for us."

8

Querida Amazonia
Beloved Amazon

(February 2, 2020)

Following the 2019 Synod of Bishops on the Pan-Amazon region, Pope Francis issued on February 2, 2020, his reflections in the form of an apostolic exhortation; it is his fifth, coming after *Evangelii Gaudium* (2013), *Amoris Laetitia* (2016), *Gaudete et Exsultate* (2018), and *Christus Vivit* (2019). Originally written in Spanish, it has been translated into at least a dozen languages. It is of modest length (16,000 words) and divided into 111 sections in four chapters. Each chapter is focused on one of "four great dreams" that the Amazon region inspires in Francis; his dreams are social, cultural, ecological, and ecclesial. Since the renewed emphasis on synods emerging in the Vatican II era, this is the first to be centered on a distinct ecological territory. This region has about 34 million inhabitants, including 3 million indigenous people from nearly 400 ethnic groups; Amazonia covers nine various countries.

Pope Francis himself provides a succinct overview of the document; he summarizes his four dreams in Section 7 of the introduction. *Social*: "I dream of an Amazon region that fights for the rights of the poor, the original peoples, and the least of our brothers and sisters, where their voices can be heard and their dignity advanced." *Cultural*: "I dream of an Amazon region that can preserve its distinctive cultural riches, where the beauty of our humanity shines forth in so many varied ways." *Ecological*: "I dream of an Amazon region that can jealously preserve its overwhelming natural beauty and the superabundant life teeming in its rivers and forests." *Ecclesial*: "I dream of Christian communities capable of generous commitment, incarnate in the Amazon region, and giving the Church new faces with Amazonian features." Uniquely, these dreams are elaborated in a very artistic and literary manner, often employing original indigenous poetry.

Several specific themes strike the perceptive reader. Francis is deeply concerned about environmental and ecological stewardship, not only for Amazonia, but for the entire world; "the mission that God has entrusted to us all [is] the protection of our common home" (19). There is an urgent need "to respect the rights of peoples and cultures" (40); this task becomes very difficult when the environment itself is severely damaged. The indigenous peoples can teach us to practice the "prophecy of contemplation" (53–57), entering into communion with the mystery of nature; we "can love it, not simply use it" (55). Francis repeatedly emphasizes the Church's task of inculturating the Gospel and capitalizing on the popular religiosity of indigenous people (77–80). One finds deep insights on the Eucharist, women, holiness, and God's revelation through "two human faces" (101), those of Jesus and Mary. Discover and enjoy another "Francis treasure!"

Querida Amazonia
Synthesis Text

Introduction

The Beloved Amazon (1). The Amazon region, with all its splendor, drama, and mystery, was the focus of the October 6–27,

2019, synod held in Rome. **The Significance of This Exhortation (2–4). (2).** Pope Francis wishes to offer his own response to the synod, proposing a brief framework for reflection, so as to guide a harmonious, creative, and fruitful reception of the synodal process. **(3).** At the same time, Francis is presenting the conclusions of the synod that arose from the direct experience of people living in that area. **(4).** Francis hopes that the insights from the synod will challenge and enrich the whole Church.

Dreams for the Amazon Region (5–7). (5). The Amazon region is a multinational (nine countries) and interconnected whole, with numerous issues and challenges; other regions of the world can learn from its efforts to address its situation. **(6).** Everything the Church offers must become incarnate in a distinctive way in each part of the world, manifested in its preaching, spirituality, and ecclesial structures. **(7).** Francis has four great dreams related to the Amazon. It is to be a region that (a) fights for the rights of the poor and disadvantaged, (b) preserves its distinctive cultural riches, (c) guards its overwhelming natural beauty, and (d) fosters Christian communities that generate deep commitment. *Note*: These four dreams provide the structure for the four chapters of this apostolic exhortation.

CHAPTER ONE: A SOCIAL DREAM

(8). The first dream envisions a region that integrates and promotes all its inhabitants; this requires both ecological and social approaches.

Injustice and Crime (9–14). (9). Colonizing interests (timber and mining industries) continue to expand both legally and illegally; this often displaces indigenous peoples. **(10).** Recently many indigenous people have migrated to the outskirts of cities; xenophobia, sexual exploitation, and human trafficking are on the rise. **(11).** The synod provided an ample diagnosis of the challenges facing the Amazon caused by timber merchants, ranchers, and other third parties; this has resulted in "a region of stolen territories." **(12).** Benedict XVI has already condemned the devastation of the Amazon basin. The rights of the original peoples and their human dignity were almost totally disregarded. **(13).** The original peoples often witnessed helplessly the destruction of their natural surroundings; the imbalance of power became enormous. **(14).** The unethical practices that harm the Amazon and its peoples should be called for what they are: *injustice and crime*. The Church cannot allow this situation to become "a new version of colonialism."

To Feel Outrage and to Beg Forgiveness (15–19). (15). Like biblical characters we need to feel outrage; we cannot become inured to evil; our social consciousness must not become dulled. Incidents of injustice and cruelty ought to provoke profound abhorrence. **(16).** Such a history of suffering and contempt does not heal easily; colonization continues in changed, disguised, and concealed forms. Always, it is a minority that profits from the poverty of the majority. **(17).** While feeling a healthy sense of indignation, we still believe it is possible to overcome the various colonizing mentalities and to build networks of solidarity and development. **(18).** One must recall that amid grave contradictions and suffering, many missionaries have come to the Amazon to bring the Gospel; the local people begged them not to leave or abandon them. **(19).** The Church renews her commitment today to the Amazonian peoples; she also asks forgiveness for the crimes committed against the native peoples. All must join together to serve the mission given by God: "the protection of our common home."

A Sense of Community (20–22). (20). Building a just society requires a capacity for fraternity, a spirit of human fellowship; it also recognizes that the relationships of people are deeply steeped in their surrounding nature. **(21).** One can sense the bewilderment and uprootedness of those forced to migrate to the cities. We must search for ways to heal these hurts and to bring serenity and meaning to those whose lives have been uprooted. **(22).** Since Christ redeemed the whole person, we seek to enter into relationship with others, pursuing justice, fraternity, and solidarity, giving impetus to the culture of encounter.

Broken Institutions (23–25). (23). Pope Francis already noted in *Laudato Sí* that society's institutions need to serve the quality of human life and environmental concerns; unfortunately, in many countries there is a relatively low level of institutional effectiveness. **(24).** In the Amazon region there is a loss of confidence in institutions and their representatives; the Amazonian peoples are not immune to corruption, ending up its principal victims. **(25).** Admittedly, some members of the Church have been part of networks of corruption (e.g., the reception of donations and other kinds of benefits).

Social Dialogue (26–27). (26). The Amazon region ought to be a place of social dialogue among its various original peoples, especially with the poor. They are our principal dialogue partners, from whom we have the most to learn. Their words, hopes, and fears are pivotal at the table of dialogue on the Amazon region. **(27).** Dialogue must have a preferential option for the poor, marginalized, and excluded; otherwise, any proposal may only be "a plan drawn up by the few for the few." "A prophetic voice must be raised," and we Christians are called to make it heard.

Chapter Two: A Cultural Dream

(28). Promoting the Amazon region seeks "to cultivate without uprooting, to foster growth without weakening identity, to be supportive without being invasive."

The Amazonian Polyhedron (29–32). (29). The Amazon region encompasses many peoples and nationalities (e.g., over 110 indigenous peoples). They are *not* uncivilized savages; they are heirs to different cultures and other forms of civilization. **(30).** The advance of colonization drove the original inhabitants into the interior; today, growing desertification forces many of them into cities. This process disrupts the cultural transmission of wisdom; cities become "a tragic scenario of discarded lives." **(31).** Each of the surviving peoples possesses its own cultural identity and unique richness (this treasure is captured in a lengthy poetic quote). **(32).** Human groupings, their lifestyles, and worldviews are as varied as the land itself; thus, unfair generalizations, simplistic arguments, and conclusions must be assiduously avoided.

Caring for Roots (33–35). (33). A "consumerist vision of human beings" diminishes the heritage of all humanity; to prevent this process of human impoverishment it is necessary to take charge of one's roots, thus allowing all to grow, flourish, and bear fruit. **(34).** For centuries cultural wisdom was handed on through "primitive storytellers"; it remains necessary that older people tell their stories, so that young people can drink deeply from this source. **(35).** Fortunately, some have begun writing down their stories, which are the bearers of precious personal, family, and collective memories. The Amazon region has also become the source of artistic, literary, musical, and cultural inspiration.

Intercultural Encounter (36–38). (36). Similar to all cultural realities, the cultures of the interior Amazon region have their limits; thus, it becomes necessary to listen to *all* of life's experiences, the positive and the negative. **(37).** Everyone needs to sit around the common table as a place of conversation and shared hopes; this dialogue enriches the cultural values of all involved, thus avoiding that a culture becomes stagnant and barren. **(38).**

This intercultural dialogue will enrich the original peoples of the Amazon region.

Endangered Cultures, Peoples at Risk (39–40). (39). Boldly, Pope Francis asserts, "The globalized economy shamelessly damages human, social, and cultural richness." The importance of the family in keeping cultures alive is undeniable. **(40).** The "quality of life" cannot be imposed from without; it must be understood within the world of symbols and customs proper to each human group.

CHAPTER THREE: AN ECOLOGICAL DREAM

(41). In a cultural reality like the Amazon region, there is a close relation between human beings and nature; thus, there is need of care for all humans as well as for the environment. An "ecology of nature" must be joined to a "human ecology" and a "social ecology." **(42).** Abusing nature is also abusing one's ancestors, brothers and sisters, creation and the Creator; it is mortgaging the future. Insightfully, the document asserts, "The land has blood, and it is bleeding; the multinationals have cut the veins of our mother Earth."

This Dream Made of Water (43–46). (43). In the Amazon region, water is queen; the rivers and streams are like veins, and water determines every form of life. **(44).** The shimmering water of the Amazon River collects and enlivens all its surroundings. **(45).** The Amazon, offspring of many rivers, is also the spinal column that creates harmony and unity. However, there is a growing fear that this source of life is slowly coming to an end. **(46).** We can turn to poets, contemplatives, and prophets to help free us from "the technocratic and consumerist paradigm that destroys nature and robs us of a truly dignified existence."

The Cry of the Amazon Region (47–52). (47). Poetry helps give voice to shared realizations that much of the Amazon and its beauty is in grave danger. **(48).** Together with the biome of the Congo and Borneo, the equilibrium of planet earth depends on the health of the Amazon region. As an ecosystem, each part is essential for the preservation of the whole. **(49).** The healthy functioning of an ecosystem requires numerous elements—for example, fungi, worms, insects, reptiles, and a wide variety of microorganisms— yet the sources of pollution are increasing. **(50).** National governments need a greater sense of responsibility; they must not capitulate to spurious local or international interests. **(51).** To protect the Amazon region, ancestral wisdom can be combined with contemporary technical knowledge; in everything the original peoples must have their voice and concerns be heard. **(52).** An enforceable legal framework that sets clear boundaries and ensures the protection of ecosystems is essential for everyone's welfare. As God's people cried out in Egypt (Ex 3:7), today the Amazon region cries out to the Creator.

The Prophecy of Contemplation (53–57). (53). If one's conscience is deadened, then evasiveness and self-destructive vices can dominate. Do such vices control the manner in which we care for planet earth? **(54).** Each year thousands of plant and animal species disappear; most of these become extinct for reasons related to human activity. **(55).** From the original peoples, we can begin to contemplate the Amazon, learning to love it and intimately feel a part of it. **(56).** We are called to awaken our God-given contemplative sense, entering into communion with nature and weeping for the Amazon region. **(57).** God calls us to be his instruments for hearing the cry of the Amazon. Thus, we will encounter in the Amazon region a *theological locus*, a space where God reveals himself.

Ecological Education and Habits (58–60). (58). A sustainable and integral ecology, one capable of bringing change, will not develop unless people change and opt for a more fraternal lifestyle. **(59)**. Many people who have an "empty heart" adopt a consumerist lifestyle; this may even lead to violence and mutual destruction. **(60)**. The Church has a valuable contribution to make, because of her value of creation, her concern for justice and for the poor, and her history of "becoming incarnate" in cultures throughout the world.

CHAPTER FOUR: AN ECCLESIAL DREAM

(61). The Church is called to journey with the people of the Amazon region, as it has done through its many plenary assemblies of the Latin American Bishops' Conference; her missionary proclamation must continue to resound. She must become a Church with an Amazonian face.

The Message That Needs to Be Heard in the Amazon Region (62–65). **(62)**. While the Church can offer various organizational and technical programs, she will also emphasize the call to faith and mission. **(63)**. An authentic option for the poor involves inviting them to friendship with the Lord; we recognize Christ in them and are aware of their God-given dignity. **(64)**. The poor have a right to hear the Gospel and experience God's love; this message was well summarized in Chapter 4 of *Christus Vivit*. **(65)**. The command to living fraternal charity summarizes the whole Gospel and is the best sign that identifies us as Christ's disciples.

Inculturation (66–69). **(66)**. The Church is called to engage in the process of inculturation, building upon the goodness found in the Amazonian cultures. She promotes the living Tradition of the Church and "is called to keep the flame alive rather than to guard its ashes." **(67)**. Saint John Paul II noted that "a faith that does not become culture is a faith not fully accepted, not fully reflected upon, not faithfully lived." **(68)**. Pope Francis recalls insights from his *Evangelii Gaudium*, emphasizing how the Gospel is to be preached in categories proper to each culture. **(69)**. The process of inculturation is a difficult but necessary journey; thus, "let us be fearless; let us not clip the wings of the Holy Spirit."

Paths of Inculturation in the Amazon Region (70–74). **(70)**. A renewed inculturation in the Amazon region requires that the Church listen to the rich insights of ancestral wisdom from pre-Columbian cultures. **(71)**. The indigenous peoples have insights into authentic living that include personal, familial, communal, and cosmic harmony; these values need to be integrated into the process of evangelization. **(72)**. Numerous forms of ecclesial outreach are needed: befriending people, listening and speaking for them, staying close to the youth and migrants, and so on. **(73)**. Authentic inculturation elevates and fulfills; it esteems indigenous mysticism and sacred wonder; it fosters a relationship with God. **(74)**. Founded on Christ's true incarnation, the Christian experience values all creatures of the material universe, taking up elements of the world and integrating them into an inculturated faith. The Eucharist is a fine example of such integration.

Social and Spiritual Inculturation (75–76). **(75)**. Inculturation includes a social dimension, incorporating human development and a commitment to the justice of God's Kingdom. **(76)**. Gospel inculturation integrates the social and spiritual, responding to people's deepest yearnings; thus, it "fully humanizes, integrally dignifies persons and peoples, and brings fulfillment to every heart and the whole of life."

Starting Points for an Amazonian Holiness (77–80). **(77)**. Inculturation initiatives will give rise to a witness of holiness with an Amazonian face; authentic holiness is attained by "each individual [culture] in his or her own way." **(78)**. An inculturated faith often possesses "certain features of popular Catholicism," enabling us "to see how the faith, once received, becomes embodied in a culture and is constantly passed on." **(79).** It is possible to appreciate that indigenous symbols and myths have spiritual meaning, and through a process of purification and maturation can result in "an inculturated spirituality." **(80).** Such a spirituality will center on the one God and Lord, while at the same time meeting the daily needs of local people.

The Inculturation of the Liturgy (81–84). (81). The sacraments "unite the divine and the cosmic, grace and creation"; they are a privileged way in which nature is taken up by God to become a means of mediating supernatural life. **(82).** The Eucharist joins heaven and earth; it embraces and penetrates all creation. Thus, as encouraged by Vatican II, it is valid to incorporate native forms of expression in song, dance, rituals, gestures, and symbols. **(83).** The practice of Sunday and Feast-day rest is encouraged, since it integrates a dimension of receptivity and gratuity into all our labors. **(84).** Since the sacraments reveal and communicate God's nearness and mercy, they must be readily accessible for the poor; they must never be refused for financial reasons or be limited by excessive rules.

Inculturation of Forms of Ministry (85–90). (85). Inculturation should increasingly be reflected in various forms of ecclesial organization and ministry, furthering the pastoral presence of the Church. **(86).** More frequent celebration of the Eucharist is needed, marked by an appreciation of Amazonian sensibilities and cultures. **(87).** The "way of shaping priestly life and ministry is not monolithic." While recognizing that Holy Orders qualifies the priest to celebrate the Eucharist, other ministerial functions can be delegated; all initiatives are ordered to the holiness of Christ's members. **(88).** Church teaching recognizes that the celebration of two sacraments (Eucharist and Penance/Reconciliation) are reserved to ordained priests. **(89).** The laity validly engage in numerous ministries (e.g., proclaiming God's Word, teaching, organizing communities, leading popular devotions, etc.), yet all need the Eucharist because it "makes the Church." **(90)**. Everyone needs to promote priestly and missionary vocations for the Amazon region.

Communities Filled with Life (91–98). **(91)**. The Eucharist signifies and realizes Church unity; it fosters communion among the variety of gifts and charisms in the Church. **(92)**. The Eucharist, the source and summit of Christian life, should result in the growth of numerous ministries (e.g., permanent deacons, religious women, and laypersons). **(93)**. Beyond seeking priestly vocations, the Church must promote a deep encounter with God's Word and a growth in holiness; this endeavor must be done on four levels: biblical, doctrinal, spiritual, and practical. **(94)**. A Church with Amazonian features requires the presence of mature and lay leaders, open to the Spirit's boldness on all levels of Church life.

(95). A "new impetus to inculturation" is needed, combining creativity, missionary boldness, sensitivity, and a strong community life. **(96)**. Base communities, an authentic expression of synodality, are central to evangelization in the Amazon region. **(97)**. Pope Francis encourages a Pan-Amazonian Ecclesial Network; this necessarily involves the local churches on the Amazonian borders. **(98)**. The Church must plan for stable communities as well as migrating peoples (to be served by itinerant missionary teams).

The Strength and Gift of Women (99–103). **(99)**. Several Amazonian communities have long preserved the faith; credit is due to many strong and generous women who baptized, catechized, prayed, and acted as missionaries. **(100)**. This experience summons us to broaden our vision; it does not imply that women should be ordained. We do not wish to clericalize women or diminish their current great contribution. **(101)**. The Lord chose to reveal his love through two human faces: the man Jesus and the woman Mary. In Mary, we realize that without women the Church would suffer and even break down. **(102).** We must continue encouraging those diverse gifts that enabled women in the Amazon region to play so active a role in society. **(103).** In a synodal Church, women should have access to positions, including ecclesial services, that do not entail Holy Orders; thus, they will continue to have a real and effective impact on the Church.

Expanding Horizons beyond Conflicts (104–105). **(104).** Probably, an effective response to current challenges of evangelization lies in transcending the "clerical divide"; new approaches should be explored. **(105).** Realistically, the Church seeks to face problems with boldness and generosity, following paths of inculturation that are broad and creative.

Ecumenical and Interreligious Coexistence (106–110). **(106).** In the Amazonian region, all believers must search for occasions to speak together, to act for the common good, and to promote the welfare of the poor; we believe the Holy Spirit can work amid differences. **(107).** Catholics possess many treasures (e.g., Scripture, Jesus, the sacraments, Mary) that we wish to share with others; we also wish to learn from the wealth of other religions. **(108).** In the true spirit of dialogue, we are open about our beliefs that unite us; we wish to avoid being swallowed up by worldly attitudes of selfishness, consumerism, and self-destructive individualism. **(109).** As Christians, we are united by faith in God and in Jesus the Savior; we are united by the fire of the Spirit, who sends us forth on mission. In addition, we are united by the new commandment and in our common struggle for peace and justice. **(110).** Thus united, we struggle together, pray and work side by side to defend the poor of the Amazon region and to care for God's work of creation.

CONCLUSION: MOTHER OF THE AMAZON REGION

(111). Francis seeks to encourage everyone to promote the advancement of the Amazon region. He directs our gaze to Mary, who reveals herself in the Amazon region in distinct ways; he prays: We ask you, Mary, to reign in the beating heart of Amazonia; show yourself the Mother of all creatures. Ask Jesus to pour out all his love on all the inhabitants; bring your Son to birth in their hearts. Mother, look upon the poor of the Amazon region. Touch the hearts of the powerful. Reign so that no one else can claim lordship over the handiwork of God. Do not abandon us in this dark hour. Amen.

9

Fratelli Tutti
On Fraternity and Social Friendship

(October 3, 2020)

On the eve of the October 4 feast of Saint Francis of Assisi, Pope Francis released his third encyclical, titled *Fratelli Tutti*. As with Francis' second encyclical, *Laudato Sí*, the Italian title is drawn from the writings of the pope's namesake, Francis of Assisi, who lived in the twelfth century and is now the patron saint of ecology. The document is lengthy (eight chapters of 43,000 words in 287 paragraphs with 288 footnotes); however, its sheer size should not eclipse its relevant and urgent message! A few of its key themes are the following: renewed human relationships on all levels of society, the call for peace and reconciliation, the renewal of politics, care for the earth our common home, more cordial relations between Christianity and Islam, and religions at the service of human solidarity.

The eight chapters of *Fratelli Tutti* can serve as a walking tour of the encyclical. First, "Dark Clouds over a Closed World" summarizes numerous challenges facing humanity today. Next, "A Stranger on the Road" is a marvelous reflection on Jesus' Good Samaritan parable. Chapter 3, "Envisioning and Engendering an Open World," outlines a vision of human solidarity. All people need "A Heart Open to the Whole World," as portrayed in chapter 4. Three chapters summarize some urgent needs of humanity today: "A Better Kind of Politics" (5), "Dialogue and Friendship in Society" (6), and "Paths of Renewed Encounter" (7). The final chapter, "Religions at the Service of Fraternity in Our World," portrays the pivotal contribution that the world's religions can make to building fraternity and defending justice in the wider society.

As we seek to grow in our faith and social commitment, we look for practical paths to make progress; certainly, reading and absorbing the deep insights of Pope Francis' writings will profoundly enrich us. Consider *Fratelli Tutti* as a vast smorgasbord of fine food; taste and savor all its rich fare. One might read a chapter a week, devote fifteen minutes to reflective meditation daily, or bring the full encyclical on your annual retreat. Whatever your choice, commit to absorbing and implementing the vision and dreams of Pope Francis on fraternity and social friendship. Truly, you will discover that we are "brothers and sisters all" (8)!

Fratelli Tutti
Synthesis Text

INTRODUCTION

(1). "*Fratelli Tutti*." With these words, Saint Francis of Assisi addressed his brothers and sisters, proposing a way of life and love that transcends various barriers, especially those of geography and distance. (2). Pope Francis notes that this saint of fraternal love, simplicity, and joy prompted him to write *Laudato Sí* and to also now write a new encyclical on fraternity and social friendship.

Without Borders (3–8). (3). A significant event in Francis' life shows his openness of heart. He journeyed to Egypt to visit the Muslim Sultan Malik-el-Kamil—even in the time of the Crusades. **(4).** Francis did not wage a war of words. He wanted to inspire a vision of a fraternal society; he himself became one of the poor and sought to live in harmony with all. Pope Francis states simply, "Francis has inspired these pages." **(5)**. Human fraternity and social friendship are concerns of Pope Francis. He takes inspiration from the Orthodox Patriarch Bartholomew and the Grand Imam Ahmad Al-Tayyeb. **(6)**. This document seeks to offer a "modest contribution" to the teaching on fraternal love. **(7)**. The Covid-19 pandemic manifested our need to cooperate more fully. **(8)**. Francis hopes to contribute to the rebirth of a universal aspiration to fraternity. "Let us dream, then, as a single human family," as brothers and sisters all.

CHAPTER ONE: DARK CLOUDS OVER A CLOSED WORLD

(9). This text is not an exhaustive analysis of current realities; it aims to simply consider trends in society that hinder the development of universal fraternity.

Shattered Dreams (10–12). **(10)**. The world has seen some movements toward various forms of integration, such as the European Union. **(11)**. However, at present, there are signs of regression (e.g., myopic and aggressive nationalism, loss of a social sense, etc.). **(12)**. Economic and financial interests appear to dominate and derail a true "opening up to the world." Truly, "as society becomes ever more globalized, it makes us neighbors, but does not make us brothers." **The End of Historical Consciousness (13–14)**. **(13)**. The current loss of a sense of history leads to further breakup. **(14)**. New forms of cultural colonization are emerging.

Lacking a Plan for Everyone (15–17). **(15)**. An effective way to dominate people is to spread despair and discouragement. Society becomes impoverished when subjected to the hubris of the powerful, who often use "slick marketing techniques" to promote their agenda. **(16)**. Although seemingly "madness" to some, a plan is needed that would set great goals for the development of the entire human family. **(17).** Caring for the world means thinking of ourselves more and more as a single family dwelling in a common home.

A "Throwaway" World (18–21). **(18).** Human persons have paramount importance. This principle applies to the poor and disabled, the "not yet useful" like the unborn, and the "no longer useful" like the elderly. **(19).** The decline in the birth rate and the marginalization of older people are forms of discarding others. **(20).** Social progress is also impeded when labor practices lead to unemployment, which, in turn, leads to the expansion of poverty. Instances of racism also continue to shame us. **(21).** While some economic policies have proven effective for growth, they have not always fostered integral human development; new forms of poverty are emerging.

Insufficiently Universal Human Rights (22–24). **(22).** By closely observing our contemporary societies, we see numerous contradictions, manifesting that, in practice, human rights are not equal for all; this reality does not reflect the innate human dignity of all. **(23).** Worldwide, the situation of women is often not on a par with that of men; frequently, they are less able to defend their rights. **(24).** A disturbing fact is that "millions of people today— children, women and men of all ages—are deprived of freedom and forced to live in conditions akin to slavery." Particularly deplorable are situations of forced abortions, kidnapping for the sale of human organs, and trafficking in persons.

Conflict and Fear (25–28). **(25).** War, terrorist attacks, racial or religious persecution, and other affronts to human dignity are, sad to say, so common that they "constitute a real 'third world war' fought piecemeal." **(26).** These realities reflect the fact that we no longer have common horizons that unite us. The human family's innate vocation to fraternity has been lost and is often replaced by a mentality of fear and mistrust. **(27).** These factors result in "the temptation to build a culture of walls, to raise walls, walls in the heart, walls on the land.... Those who raise walls will end up as slaves within the very walls they have built." **(28).** The loneliness, fear, and insecurity experienced by those who feel abandoned "creates a fertile terrain for various 'mafias.'"

Globalization and Progress without a Shared Road Map (29–31). (29). In harmony with the Grand Imam Ahmad Al-Tayyeb, Pope Francis acknowledges areas of progress. This is asserted in their joint statement, *Document on Human Fraternity for World Peace and Living Together* (February 4, 2019). **(30).** Within the human family, indifference and a sort of cynicism must be overcome by a "culture of encounter." In a word, "isolation, no; closeness, yes. Culture clash, no; culture of encounter, yes." **(31).** Indeed, "how wonderful it would be if the growth of scientific and technological innovation could come with more equality and social inclusion."

Pandemics and Other Calamities in History (32–36). (32). The worldwide Covid-19 pandemic momentarily revived the sense that we are a global community. No one is saved alone; we can only be saved together. **(33).** Simple networking does not automatically produce fraternity. Virtual reality cannot replace the "truly real." **(34).** Observing our reality, we are reminded of the well-known verse of the poet Virgil that evokes the "tears of things" and the misfortunes of life and history. **(35).** We quickly forget the lessons of history, "the teacher of life" (Cicero). When the healthcare crisis is over, will we return to feverish consumerism? **(36).** We seek to recover the shared passion to create a community of belonging and solidarity worthy of our time!

An Absence of Human Dignity on the Borders (37–41). (37). The plight of many migrants is alarming. They face war, persecution, and natural calamities at home; thus, they decide to migrate. **(38).** They experience violence, trafficking, psychological and physical abuse, and untold sufferings on their journey. Migrants have a right to emigrate and also to stay in their homeland. **(39).** Migrants possess the same intrinsic dignity as any person, yet the treatment they receive shows that they are often considered less worthy, less important, less human. **(40).** It is clear that migration will play a pivotal role in the future of our world. **(41).** While some people are hesitant and fearful with regard to migrants, this fear deprives us of the desire and the ability to encounter the other.

The Illusion of Communication (42–43). (42). People have need of the right to privacy. If digital communication invades every aspect of life, respect for others disintegrates. **(43).** Digital media can have both a positive and negative impact, yet digital connectivity alone is not enough to build bridges. **Shameless Aggression (44–46). (44).** Social aggression has found room for expansion through computers and mobile devices. **(45).** In this context, ideologies can prosper; fake news easily spreads; manipulative controls serving economic interests gain momentum. **(46).** We admit that "destructive forms of fanaticism are at times found among religious believers, including Christians." How can we contribute to the fraternity desired by our common Father?

Information without Wisdom (47–50). (47). True wisdom demands an encounter with reality; however, virtual networks may isolate us from the real world in which we are living. **(48).** The ability to listen deeply to others fosters interpersonal encounters and transcends narcissism. Francis of Assisi listened to God, the poor, the infirm, and nature; this seed planted by Francis needs to grow in our hearts. **(49).** Lack of silence and careful listening blocks the serene reflection that leads to shared wisdom. **(50).** The flood of information at our fingertips does not make for greater wisdom. Building fraternity needs persons free and open to authentic encounters.

Forms of Subjection and of Self-Contempt (51–53). (51). Prosperous countries are often proposed as cultural models for less developed nations. However, every country should be helped to grow in its own distinct way, respecting the values of its proper culture. **(52).** Destroying culture and self-esteem becomes an easy way to dominate others; it also adversely affects workable development plans. **(53).** "There is no worse form of alienation than to feel uprooted, belonging to no one." **Hope (54–55). (54).** Despite these dark clouds, this document will discuss many new paths of hope. **(55).** Pope Francis says, "I invite everyone to renewed hope.... Hope is bold.... It can open up to grand ideals that make life more beautiful and worthwhile."

Chapter Two: A Stranger on the Road

(56). While the description of the problems facing the world today is indeed challenging, one should recall the vision of the Second Vatican Council, which encouraged Christians to engage in the "joys and hopes, the grief and anguish of the people of our time" (GS 1). The parable of the Good Samaritan (Lk 19:25–37) offers us many profound insights; thus, Pope Francis devotes this entire second chapter to a meditation on this parable told by Jesus Christ 2,000 years ago.

The Context (57–62). (57). The Bible takes up the age-old issue of human relationships. It encourages us to create a culture in which we resolve our conflicts and care for one another. **(58).** The Book of Job sees our origin in the one Creator as the basis of certain common rights (Job 31:15). Saint Irenaeus uses the image of a melody to make the same point. **(59).** While earlier Jewish traditions appear to have limited the imperative of love to relationships between members of the same nation, their perspective gradually expands. **(60).** In the New Testament, the command to treat others as you would have them treat you becomes universal in scope. **(61).**

Francis next quotes eight biblical passages pertinent to the treatment of one's neighbor [Ex 22:21; 23:9; Lev 19:33–34; Deut 24:21–22; Gal 5:14; 1 Jn 2:10–11; 3:14; 4:20]. **(62).** Genuine love enables us to create one human family. Love exudes compassion and dignity.

Abandoned on the Wayside (63–68). (63). This parable notes how two persons holding important social positions passed by the injured man. The Samaritan gave assistance, sacrificing his personal time and convenience. **(64).** Francis asks us a blunt, direct, and incisive question: "Which of these persons do you identify with?" **(65).** A society is unhealthy when it has "no time to waste on other people's problems," turning its back on suffering. **(66).** The Good Samaritan shows us that the existence of every person is deeply tied to the situation of others. **(67).** This parable shows us that a true community can only be built by men and women who identify with the vulnerability of others. **(68).** Note that the parable does not indulge in abstract moralizing; it focuses us on the fact that we were created for a fulfillment that is only found in love.

A Story Constantly Retold (69–71). (69). This parable also evokes the interior struggle each of us experiences: including or excluding the wounded in society. We must also admit that we have personally imitated each of the characters in the parable. **(70).** Moments of crisis reveal there are only two kinds of people: those who care for the hurting and those who pass by. **(71).** The story of the Good Samaritan is constantly being repeated today in our world. By this parable Jesus is encouraging us to persevere in love and build a compassionate society.

The Characters of the Story (72–76). (72). Admittedly, there are various kinds of "robbers" in the world, seeking their personal gain and power. **(73).** The priest and the Levite are unconcerned passersby; many today prefer to keep a safe distance from the needy in the world. **(74).** Note that the passersby were religious. Belief in God alone is not enough to ensure that we are actually living in a way that is pleasing to God. "Paradoxically, those who claim to be unbelievers can sometimes put God's will into practice better than believers." **(75)**. Unfortunately, "robbers" often find secret allies in those who pass by and look the other way. Looking away—not getting involved—allows social injustices to continue. **(76)**. There are many "injured" in our world; we must actually touch them, not only sympathize at a safe distance.

Starting Anew (77–79). **(77)**. Each day offers new opportunities to share others' pain and to lift them up, focusing on becoming a people, a community. **(78)**. We can start from below with the same care and concern that the Samaritan showed. Real difficulties are no excuse for a glum resignation. "Let us stop feeling sorry for ourselves and acknowledge our crimes, our apathy, our lies." **(79)**. The Samaritan who stopped to help departed without expecting any recognition or gratitude; let us work with that same fraternal spirit of care and closeness to all the needy.

Neighbors without Borders (80–83). **(80)**. In the parable the lawyer asks who is his neighbor. Jesus' answer challenges us not to decide for ourselves, but rather that we manifest fraternal love to all. **(81)**. In short, we are asked to "become neighbor" by transcending current barriers. **(82)**. Note that the Samaritan assists a Judean, crossing existing cultural and religious barriers. **(83)**. These same barriers appear during Jesus' encounter with the Samaritan woman he met at the well (Jn 4:9). Indeed, there is a universal dimension in our call to love, "one that transcends all prejudices, all historical and cultural barriers, all petty interests."

The Plea of the Stranger (84–86). **(84)**. In the Gospel passage on the Last Judgment, Jesus says, "I was a stranger and you welcomed me" (Mt 25:35). Jesus could speak these words because his sensitive heart was open to the difficulties of others. **(85)**. As

Christians we believe that Christ shed his blood for each of us; thus, no one is beyond the scope of his universal love. **(86).** Pope Francis wonders aloud why it took so long for the Church to condemn slavery and various forms of violence. The social meaning of human existence and the inalienable dignity of each person need constant emphasis in catechesis and preaching.

CHAPTER THREE: ENVISAGING AND ENGENDERING AN OPEN WORLD

(87). Human beings are so made that they cannot live, develop, and find fulfillment except "in the sincere gift of self to others." We cannot know ourselves apart from encounters with other persons. Life exists where there is bonding, communion, and fraternity.

Moving beyond Ourselves (88–90). (88). In the depth of every human heart, love creates bonds and draws people out of themselves toward others. **(89).** Mature relationships move beyond small groups, even beyond family, to a broader network of relationships. We find that our hearts expand as we step out of ourselves and embrace others. **(90).** It is remarkable that many small desert communities saw that welcoming pilgrims was a sacred duty of hospitality. Saint Benedict insisted that "the poor and pilgrims be treated with utmost care and attention."

The Unique Value of Love (91–94). (91). As we grow in various moral virtues, we take into account the extent to which they foster openness and union with others. **(92).** The true spiritual stature of a person is measured by the ability to love. **(93).** Thomas Aquinas described the love made possible by God's grace as a movement toward another, whereby we consider "the beloved as somehow united to ourselves." The other is considered of great value to me. **(94).** Genuine love moves beyond a simple series of benevolent actions; it considers others of value, worthy, pleasing, and beautiful, moving beyond simple moral or physical appearances.

A Love Ever More Open (95–96). (95). Genuine love moves us to seek universal communion and thus find fulfillment. **(96).** Transcending our limitations applies to different regions and countries; we desire to form communities of brothers and sisters. **Open Societies That Integrate Everyone (97–98). (97).** Daily we make efforts to expand our circles of friends and colleagues. We are very aware of the virus of racism that can easily spread. **(98).** We always seek ways to better integrate people who may be on the peripheries (e.g., the disabled, the elderly, etc.).

Inadequate Understandings of Universal Love (99–100). (99). A genuine love capable of transcending borders in all places and contexts can be called "social friendship." The tendency to create societal categories always needs to be addressed to avoid creating "first and second-class" citizens. **(100).** Francis clarifies that he is not proposing some kind of "authoritarian and abstract universalism." The rich gifts and uniqueness of each person and each people must be treasured. Succinctly stated, "The future is not monochrome!"

Beyond a World of "Associates" (101–102). (101). We return to the parable of the Good Samaritan. Those who passed by were concerned with their duties, their social status, and their professional commitments; the wounded man on the roadside was only a distraction from their important daily duties. The Samaritan recognized a more urgent need. **(102).** How would people today react to the parable? If being a neighbor is limited only to those who serve one's goals, then "neighbor" loses its meaning; people are only "associates" with their own particular interests.

Liberty, Equality, and Fraternity (103–105). (103). Genuine fraternity, while respecting individual liberties, seeks to embody the values of reciprocity and mutual enrichment. **(104).** True equality is not achieved by an abstract proclamation that "all men and women are equal." Rather, it is the result of the conscious and careful cultivation of fraternity. **(105).** Individualism does not make us more free, more equal, more fraternal. It is important to recognize that "radical individualism is a virus that is extremely difficult to eliminate."

A Universal Love That Promotes Persons (106–111). (106). Social friendship and universal fraternity demand an acknowledgment of *the worth of every human person*, always and everywhere. **(107).** Every human being has the right to live in dignity and to develop integrally. **(108).** This principle, however, is often only partially accepted by some societies. **(109).** Some people are born into stable families and communities; however, society must assist those who do not have these advantages (e.g., the disabled, the poor, the uneducated, etc.). **(110).** However, "to claim economic freedom while real conditions bar many people from actual access to it… is to practice doublespeak." **(111).** Avoiding self-focused "individualistic" personal rights, we are called to transcend ourselves through an encounter with others.

Promoting the Moral Good (112–113). (112). Individuals and societies need to mature in the moral values that foster integral human development by practicing *benevolentia,* "willing the good" of others (cf. Gal 5:22). **(113).** There is an urgent need for an active promoting the good for ourselves and the entire human family. **The Value of Solidarity (114–117). (114).** Families are the first place where the values of love, fraternity, solidarity, and sharing are lived out and handed on. **(115).** Solidarity finds concrete expression in service and the care for others. **(116).** Solidarity means combatting the structural causes of poverty, inequality, and other evils. This virtue is often practiced by the poor themselves and many popular movements. **(117).** All people need the "spark of universal consciousness" to better care for our common home.

Re-envisaging the Social Role of Property (118–120). **(118).** The world exists for everyone; we have an obligation to ensure that every person lives with dignity. **(119).** Many early Christian thinkers (John Chrysostom, Gregory the Great) reflected on the common destination of created goods, assuring the basic needs of everyone. **(120).** Francis himself noted in *Laudato Sí*, "the Christian tradition has never recognized the right to private property as absolute or inviolable, and has stressed the social purpose of all forms of private property." The principle of the common use of created goods is the first and basic principle of the whole ethical and social order.

Rights without Borders (121–123). **(121).** No one can be excluded or have fewer rights (e.g., women). **(122).** Development must avoid the amassing of wealth by a few. The goods one has are to be administered for the benefit of all. **(123).** Business abilities are a gift from God to be directed to producing wealth and improving our world. **The Rights of Peoples (124–127).** **(124).** The common destination of all goods is a foundational principle. **(125).** This vision must guide all relations and exchanges between countries. **(126).** Legitimately acquired debts must be repaid based on conditions that do not compromise the very existence of poor countries. **(127).** Real and lasting peace is only possible if it is based on a global ethic of solidarity and cooperation.

CHAPTER FOUR: A HEART OPEN TO THE WHOLE WORLD

(128). If the conviction that all human beings are brothers and sisters is not to remain only an abstract idea without concrete embodiment, then numerous interrelated issues must be seen in a new light with concomitant responses.

Borders and Their Limits (129–132). **(129).** Complex challenges arise due to migration. All unnecessary migration ought to be avoided. Our response to migrating persons can be captured in four words: welcome, protect, promote, and integrate. **(130).** Numerous issues arise from migration (to mention only a few): visas, humanitarian corridors, documentation, unemployment, protecting minors, reuniting families. **(131).** Pathways to citizenship based on justice need to be established. Discriminatory language, such as the use of the term *minorities*, must be avoided. **(132).** A form of global governance with regard to movements of migration needs to emerge through common efforts among countries.

Reciprocal Gifts (133–136). (133). Persons coming from diverse ways of life and cultures can been seen as gifts, bringing opportunities for enrichment and integral human development. **(134).** The different cultures that have flourished over the centuries need to be preserved, lest our world be impoverished; this requires patience, trust, and open dialogue. **(135).** Pope Francis cites two experiences: Latino culture is enriching the United States; the influx of Italians and Jews has contributed to Argentinian society. **(136).** Francis and the Grand Imam Ahmad Al-Tayyeb have jointly observed that "good relations between East and West are indisputably necessary for all."

A Fruitful Exchange (137–138). (137). Mutual assistance between countries enriches everyone. "We need to develop the awareness that nowadays we are all saved together or no one is saved." **(138).** Current experience shows the world is intimately connected by globalization; this requires that all nations, rich and poor alike, have an effective voice in shared decision-making. **A Gratuitousness Open to Others (139–141). (139).** Authentic gratuitousness enables us to welcome the stranger. **(140).** Without fraternal gratuitousness, we can constantly be weighing the "cost" and be thinking, "What's in it for me?" Jesus asks us to remember, "Without cost you have received, without cost you are to give" (Mt

10:8). **(141).** "Only a social and political culture that readily and 'gratuitously' welcomes others will have a future."

Local and Universal (142). Admittedly, there is inter-action and tension between globalization and localization. This reality demands recognition that "universal fraternity and social friendship are thus two inseparable and equally vital poles in every society." **Local Flavor (143–145). (143).** Our dialogue with others is rooted in our own personal, national, and cultural identity. **(144).** This awareness gives rise to healthy and enriching exchanges. Recall the misguided attempt to build the Tower of Babel (see Gen 11:1–9). **(145).** The local and the global need not stifle each other. We recall the principle that "the whole is greater than the part, but it is also greater than the sum of the parts."

A Universal Horizon (146–150). (146). A truly healthy culture is open to the universal by its very nature; "a culture without universal values is not truly a culture." **(147).** Other cultures are not "enemies"; rather, they are differing reflections of the richness of human life. **(148).** Pope Francis constantly urges indigenous peoples to cherish their roots and ancestral cultures. Humans grow as a result of dialogue with those unlike themselves. **(149).** Peoples and cultures discover their own beauty as they enter the fabric of universal communion. **(150).** This vision brings the joyful realization that no one people, culture, or individual can achieve everything on its own.

Starting with Our Own Region (151–153). (151). A multifaceted education is needed to promote the value of love for one's neighbor and to move toward a healthy universal integration. **(152).** All rejoice when a lively sense of "neigh-borhood" is present; it provides a sense of shared identity. This attitude needs to grow among peoples in the same region. **(153).** Succinctly expressed, "No state can ensure the common good of its population if it remains isolated."

CHAPTER FIVE: A BETTER KIND OF POLITICS

(154). The development of a global community of fraternity and solidarity calls for a better kind of politics, one that is truly at the service of the common good.

Forms of Populism and Liberalism (155). Insensitivity for the vulnerable can hide behind both populism and liberalism. **Popular vs. Populist (156–162). (156).** The terms "populism" and "populist" have entered everyday communication; people and ideas are quickly labeled. **(157).** Such facile labeling becomes problematic; a better approach is to speak in terms of "people" who have shared goals and engage in a common endeavor. **(158).** The word "people" implies being part of a shared identity arising from social and cultural bonds. **(159).** There are sincere popular leaders who serve the common good; they do not exploit an unhealthy "populism" for their personal advantage. **(160).** A genuine "people" is open-ended, welcoming differences and seeking an integrated new synthesis. **(161).** The decline of genuine popular leadership is often reflected in its concern for short-term advantages. **(162).** In this context, the multifaceted issue of dignified employment is crucial, since work is an essential dimension of social life and human dignity.

The Benefits and Limits of Liberal Approaches (163–169). (163). The concepts of "people" and that of "neighbor" are not to be considered purely abstract or romantic ideas; they are to be lived in concrete communities. **(164).** Charity seeks to unite both dimensions, the abstract and the institutional, in the many actual realities of life. **(165).** Both the spirit of fraternity as well as efficient worldwide organization need to unite to resolve the problems of numerous poor people. **(166).** Francis asserts, "Everything, then, depends on our ability to see the need for a change of heart, attitudes, and lifestyles." **(167).** Quality human relationships emerge through education, upbringing, and spiritual growth; human weakness is also acknowledged. **(168)**. The marketplace alone cannot solve all problems. Theories of "trickle-down" economics do not resolve inequalities. **(169)**. What is needed is an economic model of social, political, and economic participation by all.

International Power (170–175). **(170)**. The financial crisis of 2007–2008, instead of developing a new economy more attentive to ethical principles, appears to have fostered greater individualism, less integration, and diminished freedom. **(171)**. Genuine progress can never bypass the dignity and rights of others or their social groups. **(172)**. The twenty-first century is witnessing the weakening of the power of nation-states due to the influence of transnational financial sectors. **(173)**. Reform of the United Nations Organization and international financial institutions is also needed. **(174)**. Instruments for the peaceful resolution of conflicts need strengthening. **(175)**. In line with the principle of subsidiarity, local groups and organizations often carry out commendable efforts to serve the common good.

Social and Political Charity (176). Although for many people today, politics is a distasteful word, can there be growth toward universal fraternity and social peace without a sound political life? **The Politics We Need (177–179)**. **(177)**. What is needed today is a politics that is farsighted and capable of new, integral, and interdisciplinary approaches to foster the common good. **(178)**. Setting aside "petty forms of politics focused on immediate interests," true statecraft needs to focus on high principles, authentic justice, the common good, and future generations. **(179)**. Global initiatives are needed, because the current situation cannot be resolved by piecemeal solutions or quick fixes.

Political Love (180–182). **(180)**. Seeking forms of social friendship that include everyone is not merely "utopian"; such efforts become a noble exercise of charity. Francis asks for a renewed appreciation of politics as "a lofty vocation and one of the highest forms of charity, inasmuch as it seeks the common good." **(181).** Authentic charity also finds expression in "macro-relationships: social, economic, and political." **(182).** Good politics seeks ways of building communities at every level of social life. **Effective Love (183–185). (183).** Social love is capable of inspiring new approaches to the world's problems. **(184).** Simply stated, charity is at the heart of every healthy and open society. **(185).** When the good of others is at stake, good intentions are not enough.

The Exercise of Political Love (186). It is an act of love to strive to organize and structure society so that others will not suffer or fall into poverty. **Sacrifices Born of Love (187–189). (187).** Genuine charity, which is "the spiritual heart of politics," practices a preferential love for those in greatest need. Francis notes "the importance of the principle of *subsidiarity*, which is inseparable from the principle of *solidarity*." **(188).** All possible avenues must be explored to protect the status and dignity of the human person. Numerous examples are given that degrade human dignity; Francis calls them "scourges." **(189).** World politics must address hunger; discarded food constitutes a genuine scandal. "Hunger is criminal; food is an inalienable right."

A Love That Integrates and Unites (190–192). (190). Healthy relations between peoples and nations are actually an exchange of gifts for the common good. **(191).** Various forms of fundamentalist intolerance actually damage relationships between individuals, groups, and peoples. **(192).** Pope Francis recalls that he and the Grand Imam Almad Al-Tayyeb have urged "the architects of international policy and world economy to work strenuously to spread the culture of tolerance and of living together in peace."

Fruitfulness over Results (193–197). (193). All public servants are called to practice love in their daily interpersonal relationships, seeking to provide different services, especially to the most insignificant of human beings. **(194)**. Politics needs to make room for a tender love of others. Tenderness is the path of choice for the most courageous men and women. **(195)**. For those who love, politics is not a quest for power; it becomes an act of sincere concern for others. **(196)**. It is truly laudable to place our hope in the hidden power of the seeds of goodness that are sown through public service. **(197)**. Viewed in this perspective, politics becomes a noble profession. All need to ask themselves various penetrating questions: How much love did I put into my work? What mark did I leave on the life of society? How much social peace did I sow?

CHAPTER SIX: DIALOGUE AND FRIENDSHIP IN SOCIETY

(198). The word "dialogue" includes "approaching, speaking, listening, looking at, coming to know and understand one another, and to find common ground." The patient dialogue of many generous persons keeps families and communities together.

Social Dialogue for a New Culture (199–202). (199). Constructive dialogue occurs as many rich cultural components interact; various types of culture can be mentioned: popular, university, youth, artistic, technological, economic, family, and media. **(200)**. Genuine dialogue is more than the exchange of opinions or social media posts. **(201)**. Truly, "the media's noisy potpourri of facts and opinions is often an obstacle to dialogue." **(202)**. The lack of sincere dialogue can mean that individual sectors are no longer concerned for the common good. Some may seek to manipulate the conversation for personal interests or the benefits of power.

Building Together (203–205). (203). Authentic social dialogue involves the ability to respect the other's point of view. Recall that "differences are creative; they create tension and in the resolution of tension lies humanity's progress." **(204)**. Society today needs greater interdisciplinary communication, leading to a more comprehensive, integral knowledge of reality. **(205)**. Present forms of communication should focus us on generous interpersonal encounters.

The Basis of Consensus (206–210). (206). The solution for social dialogue is *not* relativism. **(207)**. Genuine truth accepts that each human being is sacred and inviolable; this is a nonnegotiable principle. **(208)**. We must learn to unmask the various ways that the truth is manipulated, distorted, and concealed in public and private discourse. **(209)**. Experience has shown both the good of which we are capable as well as the possibility of inherent destructiveness. **(210)**. Society today needs to guard against the displacement of foundational moral reasoning.

Consensus and Truth (211–214). (211). Consensus is a dynamic reality achieved through respect of everyone; it is enriched and illumined by clear thinking, rational arguments, and diverse viewpoints coming from different fields of knowledge. **(212)**. In the search for consensus, people must not be afraid to get to the heart of many issues; this is achieved through dialogue. **(213)**. The inalienable dignity of every human person corresponds to human nature and is the basis of certain universal moral demands. **(214)**. We firmly believe that human nature as the source of ethical principles was created by God.

A New Culture (215). "Life, for all its confrontations, is the art of encounter." The growth of the "culture of encounter" seeks to transcend differences and divisions. **Encounter That Becomes Culture (216–217). (216)**. To promote a culture of encounter means that as a people we "should be passionate about meeting others, seeking points of contact, building bridges, planning a project that includes everyone." **(217)**. Social peace demands hard work and craftsmanship. It is important "to create *processes* of encounter, processes that build a people that can accept differences."

The Joy of Acknowledging Others (218–221). (218). The creation of a social covenant calls for the ability to recognize other people's right to be themselves and to be different. **(219).** If one part of society exploits all the world's goods, acting as if the poor did not exist, there will eventually be consequences, probably violence. **(220).** Authentic, profound, and enduring change is possible if it starts from the different cultures, particularly those of the poor. **(221).** A true social covenant, accepting that no one possesses the whole truth, is only made possible by fraternal love.

Recovering Kindness (222–224). (222). Consumerist individualism has fostered great injustices. **(223).** For Saint Paul, kindness is a fruit of the Holy Spirit (Gal 5:22); it is an attitude that is gentle, pleasant, and supportive, not rude or coarse. It involves speaking words of comfort, strength, consolation, and encouragement. **(224).** Kindness needs to be cultivated; it finds time to stop and be kind to others, to say, "Excuse me," "Pardon me," and "Thank you." Kindness facilitates the quest for genuine consensus and fraternity.

CHAPTER SEVEN: PATHS OF RENEWED ENCOUNTER

(225). In many parts of the world there is a need for peacemakers and concrete pathways to heal open wounds. **Starting Anew from the Truth (226–227). (226).** Promoting a renewed encounter does not mean returning to a time prior to conflicts; we seek to learn from historical realities and cultivate a "penitential memory." All peace processes require an enduring commitment. **(227).** Truth is always an inseparable companion of justice and mercy. We seek to break the cycle of violence, a pattern that only leads to more violence.

The Art and Architecture of Peace (228–232). (228). The path to peace does not mean making society blandly uniform; it endeavors to get people to collaborate in pursuing goals that benefit everyone. **(229).** Various bishops' conferences (e.g., South Africa, Korea) have asserted that peace is only achieved through dialogue, reconciliation, and mutual development. **(230).** As everyone in a family contributes to a common purpose, so also is the case with societies and nations. **(231).** Negotiation is often necessary for shaping concrete paths to peace. Admittedly, there is an "architecture" of peace as well as an "art" of peace that involves everyone. **(232).** All need to accept that peacebuilding is "an open-ended endeavor, a never-ending task."

Beginning with the Least (233–235). (233). Building social friendship requires the incorporation of all sectors of society, especially the most impoverished and vulnerable. **(234).** As the Latin American bishops have noted, "The option for the poor should lead us to friendship with the poor." **(235).** Working for tranquil social existence means never forgetting that inequality and the lack of integral human development make peace impossible.

The Value and Meaning of Forgiveness (236). Some persons are hesitant to talk of reconciliation; others think that reconciliation is a sign of weakness; still others may choose to avoid problems by ignoring injustices. **Inevitable Conflict (237–240). (237).** Forgiveness and reconciliation are central themes in Christianity and other religions. **(238).** Jesus never sanctioned violence or intolerance; instead, he told us to forgive "seventy times seven" (Mt 18:22). **(239).** The early Christian communities living in a pagan context sought to manifest patience, tolerance, and understanding. **(240).** When Jesus says that he did not come to bring peace to the world (Mt 10:34), he was speaking about discipleship and the challenges of one's decision to follow him.

Legitimate Conflict and Forgiveness (241–243). (241). While we are called to love everyone without exception, loving an oppressor does not mean allowing him to continue his abusive behavior. **(242).** The pivotal thing is not to fuel anger, which is unhealthy for all concerned. **(243).** Admittedly, it is difficult to overcome the bitter legacy of injustices; however, the small flame of anger in one's heart must be extinguished before it turns into a great blaze.

The Best Way to Move Forward (244–245). (244). Authentic reconciliation does not flee from conflict; it is pursued and achieved *within* conflict, resolving differences through dialogue and open, honest, and patient negotiation. **(245).** On numerous occasions, Francis has spoken of "a principle indispensable to the building of friendship in society: namely, that unity is greater than conflict." We look beyond our personal interests, seeking understanding and commitment that will ultimately bear much fruit.

Memory (246–249). (246). A sort of "social forgiveness" cannot be demanded from those who have suffered much unjust and cruel suffering; concomitantly, it is not possible to proclaim a "blanket reconciliation." In a word, "forgetting is never the answer." **(247).** The *Shoah* must not be forgotten; it is "the enduring symbol of the depths to which human evil can sink" if spurred by false ideologies. **(248).** Other historical realities that must not be forgotten are the atomic bombs dropped on Hiroshima and Nagasaki, persecutions, the slave trade, and other ethnic killings. **(249).** We can never move forward without remembering the past; we need to "keep alive the flame of collective conscience." Yes, we remember tragedies, but remembering goodness is also healthy.

Forgiving but Not Forgetting (250–254). (250). In the face of something that cannot and should not be forgotten for any reason, we can still forgive. Free and heartfelt forgiveness is a reflection of God's own infinite ability to forgive. **(251)**. Those who forgive without forgetting choose not to yield to the destructive forces that caused them so much suffering. **(252)**. Justice is properly sought out of love of justice itself. We seek to avoid falling into a spiral of revenge or the injustice of forgetting. **(253)**. When injustices have affected both sides, we still seek to show equal respect to every innocent victim. **(254)**. In difficult circumstances, we ask God's balm of mercy on our hearts, preparing us for the demanding but enriching path of seeking peace.

War and the Death Penalty (255). Resorting to war or the death penalty are two extreme and false answers that do not actually resolve problems. **The Injustice of War (256–262)**. **(256)**. Our world is encountering growing difficulties on the path to peace, and war is not a ghost from the past but a constant threat. **(257)**. If we want true integral human development for all, we must work tirelessly to avoid war between nations and peoples; the *Charter of the United Nations* provides fundamental guidelines fostering the global common good. **(258)**. The *Catechism of the Catholic Church* speaks of legitimate self-defense; however, the use of nuclear, chemical, or biological weapons does not fulfill the guidelines of the "just war" theory.

(259). In today's world, isolated outbreaks of war in one area affect the destinies of many countries; we are experiencing a "world war fought piecemeal." **(260)**. Saint John XXIII asserted that no one can maintain that war is a fit instrument to repair the violation of justice. We also admit that opportunities for peace offered by the end of the Cold War were missed. **(261)**. Every war leaves our world worse than it was before. Victims of war cannot be simply viewed as "collateral damage." **(262)**. The threat to use nuclear, chemical, or biological weapons cannot be justified as a valid "deterrent." Humanity is challenged to totally eliminate nuclear weapons.

The Death Penalty (263–270). (263). John Paul II clearly stated that the death penalty cannot be justified from a moral standpoint. Pope Francis states, "The death penalty is inadmissible"; the Church is firmly committed to calling for its abolition worldwide. **(264).** There is the need for authorities to impose penalties on evildoers, commensurate with the seriousness of the crime. **(265).** From the earliest centuries of the Church, various writers opposed the death penalty (e.g., Lactantius, Pope Nicolas I, and Saint Augustine). **(266).** Various dangerous practices seem to be growing in some countries today (e.g., preventive custody, imprisonment without trial, and use of the death penalty).

(267). States have a variety of legitimate means to protect people from an unjust aggressor, without resorting to capital punishment or extrajudicial and extralegal executions. **(268).** "All Christians and people of goodwill are today called to work not only for the abolition of the death penalty, legal or illegal, in all its forms." **(269).** We must keep in mind that "not even a murderer loses his personal dignity, and God himself pledges to guarantee this." **(270).** Pope Francis requests that Christians who remain hesitant on these points consider the teachings of the Scriptures (Is 2:4; Mt 26:52; Gen 9:5–6).

CHAPTER EIGHT: RELIGIONS AT THE SERVICE OF FRATERNITY IN OUR WORLD

(271). The world's various religions, based on their respect for each human being as a child of God, can contribute significantly to building fraternity and defending justice in society.

The Ultimate Foundation (272–276). (272). As believers, we are convinced that, without an openness to the Father, there will be no solid and stable reasons for an appeal to fraternity. **(273).** If one does not acknowledge transcendent truth, then the force

of power takes over and totalitarianism begins to emerge. **(274).**
When ideology attempts to remove God from society, that society
ends up adoring idols. Immense suffering is caused by the denial
of freedom of conscience and religious freedom. **(275).** There are
several important causes of the crises of the modern world: a desen-
sitized human conscience, a distancing from religious values, and
the prevailing individualism accompanied by materialistic philoso-
phies. **(276).** Thus, the Church, while respecting the autonomy of
political life, does not restrict her mission to the private sphere. She
does not claim to compete with earthly powers; she aims to be a
home with open doors.

Christian Identity (277–280). (277). The Church esteems
God's workings in other religions, never rejecting what is true and
holy in these faiths. The Gospel of Jesus Christ serves as a wellspring
of human dignity and fraternity. **(278).** The Church is called to
take root everywhere; this is what it means to be "catholic." She
recognizes the universal motherhood of Mary. **(279).** Whether
the Church is a minority or majority, she seeks religious freedom,
both for herself and for all other religions. **(280).** In addition, the
Church desires to act ecumenically, thus offering common witness
to God's love for all people and better serving all humanity.

Religions and Violence (281–284). (281). A journey of
peace is possible between all religions; its point of departure is God's
way of seeing things. **(282).** As believers we seek occasions to speak
and act together for the common good and the promotion of the
poor. Worship of God and love of neighbor are the essentials. **(283).**
The sacredness of life remains foundational; thus, terrorism must be
condemned in all its forms and expressions. **(284).** We are called
to be true people of dialogue and artisans of peace, seeking to open
pathways of dialogue.

An Appeal (285). Pope Francis recalls his fraternal meeting with the Grand Imam Ahmad Al-Tayyeb in Abu Dhabi in 2019, where they appealed for the adoption of a culture of dialogue as the pathway forward for humanity. They expressed their concern for various groups: all human beings, innocent human life, the poor and marginalized, orphans, widows, and refugees; they made their appeal in terms of human fraternity, freedom, justice, and mercy, and in the name of God.

Conclusion (286–287). (286). Pope Francis notes that these pages of reflection on universal fraternity were particularly inspired by Saint Francis of Assisi as well as by several non-Catholics, such as Martin Luther King, Desmond Tutu, and Mahatma Gandhi. **(287).** Francis also drew inspiration from Charles de Foucauld, who strove to be "the universal brother" to everyone. Two prayers conclude *Fratelli Tutti*. The "Prayer to the Creator" expresses a dream of fraternal encounter of all peoples. The "Ecumenical Christian Prayer," imploring each person of the Trinity, seeks growth in fraternal love within "the one humanity that God so loves."

10

Desiderio Desideravi
The Liturgical Formation of the People of God

(June 29, 2022)

Pope Francis has given the entire Church a precious gift, calling for the rediscovery of the beauty of the liturgy and its central importance in the life of the Church. Issued on the feast of Saints Peter and Paul (June 29, 2022), this medium-length apostolic letter (sixty-five paragraphs and about 11,000 words) is the pope's second document on the liturgy, following his 2021 *Traditionis Custodes*, which sought to place limits on use of the pre–Vatican II liturgy by groups opposed to the conciliar reform. This present letter is a powerful teaching document and a text for meditation; it reveals the deep liturgical and spiritual insights of Pope Francis that emerge from his many decades of living and celebrating the Paschal Mystery. For Francis— and everyone—to participate "at Eucharist is to be plunged into the furnace of God's love" (57).

One may view the document as having the following three major topics or sections: liturgy in the life of the Church (2–26), the need for serious and vital liturgical formation (27–47), and *ars celebrandi*, the art of celebrating (48–60); there is also a brief introduction and conclusion. Part 1 provides a scriptural foundation, a theology of the liturgy, some current difficulties, and the challenge to "live" the liturgy in daily life. Part 2 beautifully presents the liturgical renewal of the Second Vatican Council and its foundational role in the Church's life; here Francis eloquently connects the acceptance of the renewed liturgy with the very acceptance of the Council itself. Thus, one understands the urgent need for a deep, ongoing liturgical formation for all members of the Church. Part 3 on the art of celebrating presents numerous pivotal themes; some examples are: celebrating is an "art"; it requires "consistent application" and a deeper appreciation of symbols; all are to enter into the action of the Holy Spirit forming the Christian community at prayer; moments of silence are essential.

In addition to fostering a deeper appreciation of the riches of the liturgy, another crucial topic emerges at various points in the document: full acceptance of the entire corpus of Church teaching found in the sixteen documents of Vatican II. Emphatically, Francis asserts that there can be no retreat "to that ritual from which the Council fathers, *cum Petro et sub Petro* [with Peter and under Peter] felt the need to reform, approving [the revised liturgy] under the guidance of the Holy Spirit and following their consciences as pastors" (61). The pope also notes that an ecumenical council like Vatican II "is the highest expression of synodality in the Church" (29). Clearly, speaking from the heart, Francis asks us "to listen together to what the Spirit is saying to the Church. Let us safeguard our communion. Let us continue to be astonished at the beauty of the Liturgy" (65)!

Desiderio Desideravi
Synthesis Text

INTRODUCTION

(1). Pope Francis begins by quoting Jesus' words at the beginning of the Last Supper, expressing his desire to eat the Paschal meal with his disciples (Lk 22:15). Then Francis says he is writing this letter to share with all in the Church "some reflections on the liturgy, a dimension fundamental for the life of the Church."

The Liturgy: The "Today" of Salvation History (2–9). (2). The quoted words of Jesus in Luke 22:15 can serve to assist us in intuiting the depth of love of the persons of the Holy Trinity for us. **(3).** Peter and John, who prepared the Passover meal, are present but unaware of what is to happen—yet they are disposed to receive a special gift, a gift that will be entrusted to the Apostles so that it can be carried to all humanity. **(4).** All were invitees; no one had earned a place at that supper, a meal of "absolute newness" and "absolute originality," a meal to be repeated and shared with all peoples until Jesus returns again. **(5).** Since all are invited to this supper, the Church cannot rest until the invitation has been extended to all through the implementation of the Church's "missionary option," the fervent dream of Pope Francis highlighted in *Evangelii Gaudium* (27).

(6). Before our response to Jesus' invitation, he has already expressed his desire for us; this same desire precedes our every reception of his body and blood in communion. **(7).** The content of the bread broken is "the cross of Jesus," "his sacrifice of obedience out of love for the Father," his "act of perfect worship." Only in the gesture of the breaking of the bread do Jesus' own disciples come to "see" the risen One and once again believe. **(8).** Our own encounter with the living Jesus comes through the Christian community that follows the Lord's command: "Do this in memory of me." **(9).** Through the Eucharist and all the sacraments, we experience an authentic encounter with Jesus, truly seeing and touching him, the Incarnate Word of God.

The Liturgy: Place of Encounter with Christ (10–13). (10). If the resurrection were only a concept, idea, or thought, then we could have no true encounter with Christ. Through the incarnation, the Trinity opened to humans a pathway to communion. **(11).** In the Eucharist and all the sacraments, we are guaranteed the possibility of truly encountering the Lord Jesus and his Paschal Mystery. **(12).** Through Baptism, which is "not magic," we are plunged into Christ's passion, death, resurrection, and ascension, the Lord's "Paschal deed." **(13).** Francis narrates the numerous wonderful ways that Jesus used water for his saving work. Water reflects God's saving action, extending from the creation of water (Gen 1:2) to the water that flowed from Christ's pierced side (Jn 19:34).

The Church: Sacrament of the Body of Christ (14–15). (14). In *Sacrosanctum Concilium* (5), the Vatican II document on the liturgy, we are reminded that the wondrous sacrament of the whole Church was born from the side of Christ. **(15).** Incorporation into the Church enables us to live the fullness of the worship of God. Francis asserts, "The subject acting in the Liturgy is always and only Christ-Church, the mystical Body of Christ."

The Theological Sense of the Liturgy (16). The Second Vatican Council and the liturgical movement promoted the rediscovery of the theological understanding of the liturgy and its importance in the life of the Church, promoting its "full, conscious, active, and fruitful celebration." In the words of Saint Augustine, the Eucharist is "the sacrament of mercy, the sign of unity, and bond of charity."

The Liturgy: Antidote for the Poison of Spiritual Worldliness (17–20). (17). Already in *Evangelii Gaudium* (93–97), Francis warned against "spiritual worldliness," a dangerous temptation for the Church. This challenge comes in two forms: Gnosticism (imprisonment in one's own thoughts and feelings) and neo-Pelagianism (cancellation of the role of God's grace in salvation); both are "distorted forms of Christianity." **(18).** The liturgy is the most effective antidote against these poisons. **(19).**

If Gnosticism intoxicates us with the poison of subjectivism, the liturgy asserts the unity of all the faithful. **(20).** If neo-Pelagianism intoxicates us with the presumption of personally earned salvation, the liturgy reminds us that our only salvation is Christ's cross (cf. Gal 6:14).

Rediscovering Daily the Beauty of the Truth of the Christian Celebration (21–23). (21). Daily celebration of the liturgy is required to rediscover its beauty and inner power, to experience its transformative dimensions in our lives. **(22).** The continual rediscovery of the beauty of the liturgy is not primarily concerned with exterior observance or strict fidelity to the rubrics; this would confuse what is essential with a certain functionalism. **(23).** Yet the various "practical" aspects of the celebration and the designated rubrics should receive careful attention.

Amazement before the Paschal Mystery: An Essential Part of the Liturgical Act (24–26). (24). We seek to grow in our astonishment that the Paschal Mystery is rendered present to us in the concreteness of sacramental signs, acknowledging that the encounter with God is not the fruit of our individual interior searching; it is a beautiful gift that is freely given to us. **(25).** Our astonishment at the Paschal Mystery means marveling at God's salvific plan revealed in the Paschal deed of Jesus (cf. Eph 1:3–14). The vague expression "sense of mystery" is not to be used negatively against the liturgical reforms of Vatican II. **(26).** Wonder remains an essential part of the liturgical act, transmitted through the power of symbolic gestures.

The Need for a Serious and Vital Liturgical Formation (27–47). It is most noteworthy that Pope Francis devotes twenty-one numbers to this particular topic (one-third of the entire document). **(27).** The primary objective of the Council's liturgical reform was the recovery of the capacity by Christians today to live completely the liturgical action. **(28).** Postmodernity people often

experience being "lost," due to heightened individualism and subjectivism. **(29)**. To appreciate the renewal of Vatican II, one must
read in harmony all its four great constitutions: *Lumen Gentium*
(Church), *Dei Verbum* (Revelation), *Gaudium et Spes* (Church in
the modern world), and *Sacrosanctum Concilium* (Liturgy). Recall
that the ecumenical council, the highest expression of synodality in
the Church, began its reflection with the liturgy.

(30). Concluding the second session of the Council in 1963,
Paul VI promulgated the liturgy document and noted that the
liturgy is the first source of our communion with God, the first
school of the spiritual life, our first gift to Christian people, and a
primary invitation to the human race. **(31)**. Given the centrality of
the liturgy, Francis bluntly says, "I do not see how it is possible to say
that one recognizes the validity of the Council…, and at the same
time not to accept the liturgical reform born out of *Sacrosanctum
Concilium*." The pope asserts, "We are in need of a serious and
dynamic liturgical formation." **(32)**. From the cenacle in Jerusalem,
the Church is born on Pentecost morning, becoming "the initial cell
of the new humanity."

(33). The Eucharistic celebration becomes the privileged place,
though not the only one, of an encounter with the risen Lord. **(34)**.
Genuine liturgical formation is fundamental; Romano Guardini
declares that without liturgical formation, "ritual and textual reforms
won't help much." Francis seeks to offer some "starting points for
reflection" on "formation for the Liturgy and formation by the
Liturgy." **(35)**. The Church needs to find appropriate channels for
liturgical formation of the faithful, so that their knowledge of the
theological sense of the liturgy can increase.

(36). Considering the regular rhythm of the Church's assemblies, ordained ministers carry out an important pastoral function
for the baptized faithful. Importantly, we recall that "it is the

Church, the Body of Christ, that is the celebrating subject and not just the priest." The entire assembly can take to heart the words spoken to the priest at ordination: "Understand what you will do, imitate what you will celebrate, and conform your life to the mystery of the Lord's Cross." **(37).** Seminary liturgical studies are to be integrated in the entire corpus of theology. Insightfully, Francis notes that "a celebration that does not evangelize is not authentic, just as a proclamation that does not lead to an encounter with the risen Lord in the celebration is not authentic."

(38). Liturgical formation is not something that is acquired once and for all; permanent formation for everyone opens all to a deeper sense of wonder. **(39).** A genuine experience of liturgical celebration fosters true communion with the mystery of God; thus, liturgy is not something that is grasped mentally, but a relationship that touches all of life. **(40).** Liturgical formation aims to enrich each person in one's unique vocation, fostering a deeper encounter with the person of Christ.

(41). Reflecting on the nature of liturgy, it becomes clear that all is to be focused on the decisive question for our lives: a deep knowledge of the mystery of Christ. As Leo the Great writes, "Our participation in the Body and Blood of Christ has no other end than to make us become that which we eat." **(42).** The liturgy is done in a sacramental and incarnational manner, incorporating many material elements from all of creation, all fruit of the earth and work of human hands. **(43).** The liturgy gives glory to God, because it allows us to see God in the celebration of the mysteries and to draw life from his Passover. As Saint Irenaeus noted, "The glory of God is humans [man] fully alive; the life of humans [man] consists in seeing God."

(44). Guardini has asserted that the first task of liturgical formation is to enable people to again be capable of symbols, a very challenging task as Pope Francis notes, "because modern man has become illiterate, no longer able to read symbols." This leads to not knowing God and not knowing ourselves. We no longer have the gaze of Saint Francis of Assisi, who, for example, grasped the symbolic value of created things, addressing "brother sun" and "sister moon." Such a vision is fundamental; "it is how the Holy Trinity chose to reach us through the flesh of the Word."

(45). "The question I want to pose is," as Francis writes, "how can we become once again capable of symbols? How can we again know how to read them and be able to live them?" **(46).** "Above all, we must reacquire confidence about creation." This means seeing the many elements of creation with an incarnational perspective, so they can become "instruments of salvation, vehicles of the Spirit, channels of grace." Clearly, there is a vast distance between this vision and one that is overly materialistic or one that is predominantly spiritualistic.

(47). Another decisive question is the education necessary to be able to acquire the interior attitude that will facilitate both the understanding and use of liturgical symbols. Francis uses a very concrete pastoral image to communicate his point; he describes the value of how parents, grandparents, pastors, and catechists teach children to pray, using the sign of the cross and tracing it with one's own hand. That very gesture forms the child and forms his or her personal faith, initiating the child into symbolic language. We must never "be robbed of such richness!"

Ars Celebrandi **(48–60). (48).** One way of fostering the understanding of symbols in the liturgy centers on the *ars celebrandi*, the art of celebrating. It should lead people into a deeper sense of what is happening during the celebration. Francis bluntly states that celebration can never be reduced to either "a rubrical mechanism" or a "wild creativity without rules."

(49). An authentic *ars celebrandi* requires different kinds of knowledge. First, one needs to appreciate how, in the dynamism of the liturgy, the Paschal Mystery is made a present reality. Then it is necessary to recognize how the Holy Spirit acts in every celebration; this includes a correct understanding of inculturation. Finally, it is necessary to appreciate "the dynamics of symbolic language, its particular nature, its efficacy."

(50). The art of celebration requires consistent application; it cannot be improvised. All dimensions of the celebration must be at the service of the liturgy and the action of the Holy Spirit. We need to regain a deep sense of the art and style of praying. (51). These reflections do not apply only to the ordained ministers, but to the entire assembly that participates in the celebration as one body. (52). In the ritual act of the entire community, "silence occupies a place of absolute importance." Silence is an important symbol of the presence and action of the Holy Spirit. (53). Every gesture and word (e.g., kneeling, bowing the head, striking the breast) contributes to fostering the genuine art of celebrating the liturgy.

(54). Francis enumerates various "styles" or "models" that are certainly *inadequate*: "rigid austerity or an exasperating creativity, a spiritualized mysticism or a practical functionalism, a rushed briskness or an overemphasized slowness, a sloppy carelessness or an excessive finickiness, a superabundant friendliness or priestly impassibility." These behaviors are present, but not overly widespread; they appear to have a common root: the celebrant's desire to be the center of attention.

(55). Among many other elements that could be mentioned, Francis calls attention to "the demanding duty of preaching the homily" (a topic he addressed extensively in *Evangelii Gaudium* 135–144). (56). In the Sacrament of Holy Orders, priests have received the Holy Spirit's gift to preside in the celebrating assembly, a gift that should continue to form the priest. **(57).** Vatican II noted that the ordained minister is one of the types of presence of the Lord in the assembly. This profound reality immerses the priest in "Jesus' burning heart of love and in the heart of each of the faithful." Thus, "to preside at Eucharist is to be plunged into the furnace of God's love."

(58). When the early Christian community broke bread following the Lord's command, they did so under the gaze of Mary (Acts 1:14). As Mary protected the Word made flesh in her womb, she now protects those being formed in the womb of the Church that protects the body of her son. **(59).** Francis asserts that the priest should allow the Holy Spirit to form him, completing the work begun at his ordination. He should preside in the Eucharistic assembly, fully aware of being a sinner and with the attitude of true humility.

(60). The priest himself is formed by presiding at the liturgy; he "does not rob attention from the centrality of the altar." He is being formed in humility; he cannot rely on himself for this ministry entrusted to him. The words and actions of the liturgy are to give shape and form to his inner person. In the Eucharistic prayer, "in which all of the baptized participate by listening *with reverence and in silence* and intervening with the acclamations," the presider enables the Father's offering of his Son in the Last Supper to become truly present. The priest "cannot recount the Last Supper to the Father without himself becoming a participant in it!" Thus, it is clear that "the priest is continually formed by the action of the celebration."

Conclusion (61–65). (61). On a personal note, Pope Francis says that in this letter he wanted to share some reflections drawn from the wellspring of Christian spirituality, enabling all to grasp the intimate bond between the Council's liturgy document and all sixteen of the Vatican II documents. Forcefully, Francis asserts that the Church "cannot go back to that ritual form which the

Council fathers, *cum Petro et sub Petro*, felt the need to reform, approving under the guidance of the Holy Spirit and following their consciences as pastors, the principles from which was born the reform." Francis continues, "As I have already written, I intend that this unity be re-established in the whole Church of the Roman Rite."

(62). This letter seeks to rekindle "our wonder for the beauty of the truth of the Christian celebration" and to assert "the necessity of an authentic liturgical formation," allowing all to be formed in joy and in communion. (63). Francis invites everyone to rediscover the meaning of the liturgical year and the Lord's Day. (64). These two sources will facilitate our knowledge of and insertion into the mystery of Christ, as we await His second coming.

(65). Sunday will be retained as a precept by the Church, since before being a precept, it is "a gift that God makes for his people." Pope Francis appeals, "Let us abandon our polemics to listen together to what the Spirit is saying to the Church. Let us safeguard our communion. Let us continue to be astonished at the beauty of the Liturgy.... All this under the gaze of Mary, Mother of the Church." As an addendum, a portion of Francis of Assisi's letter to the entire order is attached; the section deals with the Eucharist. Francis writes, "The Lord of the universe, God and the Son of God, so humbles Himself that for our salvation, He hides Himself under an ordinary piece of bread! Brothers, look at the humility of God, and pour out your hearts before Him!"